Christ Without a Flag

Spirituality and Society

Christ Without a Flag

GRAHAM JOSEPH HILL

Eagna Publishing • Sydney, Australia

Published by: Eagna Publishing (Sydney, Australia)
eagnapublishing@icloud.com
Cover and interior design: Graham Joseph Hill
www.grahamjosephhill.com

paperback isbn: 978-1-7641791-8-8
ebook isbn: 978-1-7641791-9-5
version number: 2025-11-13

NATIONAL LIBRARY OF AUSTRALIA

A catalogue record for this book is available from the National Library of Australia

Contents

Introduction: The Cross Beyond the Flag

The world is burning with symbols. Nations lift their banners high, crowds chant beneath them, and too often, faith itself is wrapped in cloth not of heaven's making. The cross is hoisted beside the flag, and the name of Christ is invoked to bless violence, justify exclusion, and sanctify power.

Yet the gospel refuses such captivity. The One who died outside the city walls (unclaimed by state or empire) calls us to a kingdom without borders, a community beyond nationalism, and a love unconfined by allegiance to any earthly banner.

This book was born in that tension. It gathers reflections written across seasons of war, migration, protest, and political fracture, each asking what it means to follow Jesus when religion and nationalism conspire, when compassion grows weary, and when truth bends beneath the weight of ideology. Together, these chapters form a spiritual map for discipleship in an age of flags and fractures, tracing the shape of a cruciform life amid the idols of our time.

At the heart of it all is the cross: a scandal to empire, a rebuke to every form of domination, a sign of God's boundless empathy. In Gaza's ruins, the cross weeps with every grieving mother. At the border fences, it stands with the undocumented and displaced. In the shadows of history, it bears the scars of the enslaved and the silenced. In the streets of protest and prayer, it calls for justice rooted not in rage but in love. And in the toxic swirl of political contempt, it offers a cruciform revolution: to love even our adversaries, to see the divine image in every face, to rebuild a common life where mercy outshines victory.

The chapters that follow were first written for a community of readers yearning for depth in a superficial age. They were shared as meditations on my Substack, *Spirituality and Society with Hilly*, then gathered here as a single act of witness. They name the idols that masquerade as faith (nationalism, violence, racism, greed) and invite us to unlearn their liturgies. Yet this isn't a book of despair. Beneath every lament runs a deeper current of hope: that Christ still walks among the ruins, that grace still rises from the dust, and that the Spirit still calls us beyond fear into freedom.

To follow Christ without a flag is to live with a holy dislocation: to be in the world but not owned by its empires; to serve nations while belonging to none; to bear wounds that become wells of compassion; to embody a love strong enough to heal the fractures of our age.

So, take these pages as a pilgrimage of conscience and faith. Let them disturb where we've grown comfortable and comfort where we've grown cynical. The call of the gospel has never changed: not to wield power, but to wash feet; not to defend God, but to reveal love; not to raise a flag, but to lift a cross.

Here, at the intersection of faith and nation, empire and compassion, violence and peace, the Spirit of Christ poses a timeless question:

Whose kingdom will we serve?

PART I—FAITH IN THE FURNACE: CONFLICT, COMPASSION, AND WITNESS

Part 1 explores how discipleship is tested in the fires of war, displacement, and political polarization. Here, faith learns to resist empire by practicing mercy, truth, and peace.

1. Between Two Tears: Christian Spirituality and the Israel-Gaza War

This isn't a post for comfort. This is a post for witness. The Israel–Gaza war is a wound that bleeds on both sides: blood that calls us to lament, not slogans. Children starve in Gaza, hostages lie in captivity, cities crumble, lives vanish. Yet the suffering isn't one-sided. Israelis live in the shadow of rocket fire, trauma in shelters, grief at family tables. Here lies a tragedy that refuses simple answers.

"The cross holds no nation; it holds brokenness, and it holds both Israelis and Palestinians."

As Christians, our faith bids us to stand in the crack where grief meets hope. We mustn't stand for any violence, but for a vision of people made in the divine image. The cross holds no nation; it holds brokenness, and it holds both Israelis and Palestinians.

The Spiritual Form of Lament

Christian spiritual traditions teach us to grieve beneath the noise. In our liturgies, we call it lament: naming crying children, nameless victims, nameless perpetrators.[1] We hold the cries of Gazan mothers alongside Israeli survivors. We name Hamas' kidnapping of civilians as evil (terror frozen in ideology), and we also name Israel's actions leading to famine, blockades, death, and forced displacement as shocking and wrong. We resist reduction, because the cross resists binary thinking: failure and hope exist side by side.

---

[1] Brueggemann, *The Message of the Psalm*, especially 52–66.

In Christ, God entered history with divine vulnerability.[2] Jesus refused to dodge suffering; instead brought healing. Our spirituality must do the same: weeping with those who weep, refusing to gloss over suffering because we belong neither to clique nor creed, but to the suffering, crucified God who calls us to the way of wound-bearing love.

Truth Without Partiality

Some truths are unavoidable: Hamas kidnapped and violated civilians (women, children, and elders) as hostages. That act demands condemnation. Hamas's cruelty risked a deadly escalation. Israel's military campaign unleashed starvation, trauma, death, and destabilization in Gaza, mostly among innocent civilians, many of them children. Blockaded cities, bombed neighborhoods, and shortages of water, medicine, and fuel: this too demands moral clarity and outcry. We can't apologize for truth: and yet we must not weaponize it. We must speak truth rooted in lament, not in tribal vindication.

Christian spiritual tradition holds that justice without mercy is hollow, and mercy without justice is facile.[3] In prayer, we carry both the names of the held Israeli hostage and the names of the Palestinians starved and cut off from life. We resist political ideologies that confine truth to a banner. We can name Hamas's violence and Israel's disproportionate tactics, but also God's boundless sorrow for every single life lost.

Prayer for Both Sides

Our prayer models our spirituality. We pray for Israeli families whose loved ones are missing: in darkness, fear, and uncertainty. We pray for Gazan mothers who rise hungry, whose children's futures are obliterated. We pray for militants who surrendered to ignorance and hate. We pray for soldiers who obeyed commands even as conscience thundered warning. We pray for regional leaders (some corrupt, some desperate)

---

2 Moltmann, *The Crucified God*, 276–90.
3 Wolterstorff, *Justice in Love*, 119–34.

5

who perpetuate cycles of violence. We remember hostages taken, hostages freed, and lives unreturned.

This isn't a prayer of neutrality, but one of presence. It's not the prayer of naivete but of trust that the Spirit transforms even unbeaten stones. It's the transformational prayer that refuses to let us dehumanize people on any side of history or conflict.

The Cross as a Way of Action

What does cruciform spirituality look like here? It walks differently. It looks like support for humanitarian corridors and ceasefires: not ideological debates, but corridors where aid flows, water flows, hope flows. It looks like pressuring governments to open windows for water, food, and medicine, without strings attached. It looks like volunteering for relief efforts, supporting refugee housing, and welcoming displaced people.

Cruciform ethics doesn't shy from calling out abuses (kidnapping, rape, murder, torture, unjust imprisonment, collective punishment, starvation, ethnic cleansing, genocide, and siege tactics), but it does so without rhetorical weaponry. We call wrong "wrong," yet promote peace. We demand accountability and also forgive reality's frailty. We show solidarity with both Israeli civilians who buried their children and Gazans who bury their children after another night of bombs and starvation.

The church mustn't be a chaplain to the powerful but a sanctuary for the broken. We don't bless bombs. We bless bread. We don't sanctify oppression. We wash feet.

The gospel will always be scandalous to those who love violence, nation, and power more than service, love, reconciliation, and truth. It blesses the humble and vulnerable, not those wielding power for personal or ideological gain. It crucifies pride and resurrects love.

Prophetic love dares to grieve. It weeps for the children buried beneath rubble, the refugee pushed aside, the earth gasping for breath. Lament is the beginning of justice. But it doesn't end in tears. True lament becomes speech, and speech becomes action. The weeping disciple of Jesus rises to confront kings, systems, and silence. Grief cracks the heart open wide enough to carry courage.

"We don't bless bombs. We bless bread. We don't sanctify oppression. We wash feet."

This kind of prophetic love means we refuse to turn away from suffering, no matter whose story it is. Grief draws us into deep compassion for immigrants fleeing danger, refugees without a home, the homeless sleeping in doorways, those trapped in poverty or addiction, and families of Israeli hostages longing for return. It also opens our eyes to the staggering crisis in Gaza, where over 1.1 million people now face starvation. Lament doesn't leave us in silence; it calls us to raise our voice and act, to protect life, demand justice, and live out a love that refuses to choose between victims. Compassion rooted in grief will constantly speak, and it will never stop moving toward those who are wounded.

"Grief cracks the heart open wide enough to carry courage."

Beyond Bunker Mentalities

Nationalism shrinks the heart. Tribal identity makes vacuums in compassion. Yet resurrection rises where walls fall. The risen Christ doesn't wear a flag. Followers of that example cross borders, break bread, sit with strangers, and lose the language of siege.

In Christian spiritual theology, we follow a crucified stranger and worship a risen alien. The risen One has no fortress: only wounds.[4] Therefore, Christianity shouldn't be conflated with patriotism or religious pride. The cross refuses alliances with empire. Our loyalty is to wounds that heal, not to narratives that bind.

---

[4] Merton, *New Seeds of Contemplation*, especially chapters 10–12.

7

The Hidden Work of Hope

While bombs fall, hope arms itself with compassion. It reaches into the rubble, feeding children and parents who starve and weep. It plants micro-gardens in abandoned courtyards, teaching flowers to bloom in bombed-out soil. It creates classrooms in tents, caring for children who carry trauma like backpacks.

Mystical tradition calls us to hope that "blossoms in ashes."[5] Our faith says the tomb opened not just for Christ, but for every grieving heart. Our action says: we resist mass despair by carrying warmth: in letters to hostages, in support for refugees in Egypt, and in solidarity with peace activists, aid workers, and medical staff who are silenced, suffering, and hungry in their camps.

Spiritual Communities as Midwifery of Peace

Churches aren't just places of worship; they're clinics of the sorrowing soul. Faith communities worldwide can host justice vigils, radical feasts (with tables open to Jews, Palestinians, and others), and bilingual, interreligious, and ecumenical prayers.

We can build networks of support: a church in Amman or Tel Aviv sending food to Gazan families starving and gathering ashes; a church in Bethlehem or East Jerusalem offering guided retreats for Israeli PTSD survivors. These actions bear witness beyond politics: they're spiritual sacraments incarnated.

Towards Resurrection Ethics

Resurrection will never mean forgetting. But it does mean choosing life in the middle. Resurrection ethics affirms life (hesitantly, courageously, and tear-stained). It makes a table in the ruin, calling strangers and old enemies to feast on forgiveness. It invites former hostages and former prisoners to share cups of water, because union isn't compromise; it's revelation.

---

[5] Isaiah 61:3.

Historically, orthodox Christianity affirms the resurrection as a bodily return. We proclaim with confidence: hope isn't vapor. The promises rooted in the resurrection power of Christ still hold true: the Creator God will restore all creation and bring peace. Enmity will end. Every tear will be wiped. No bullet or bomb can annihilate divine intention.

The Courage to Speak and the Call to See

Christian spirituality isn't passive in the face of injustice. It doesn't close its eyes or hold its tongue when lives are shattered, or when power turns violent. At the heart of the gospel is the conviction that to love truthfully is to speak boldly. The Spirit that hovered over creation now stirs within disciples to cry out, not in rage, but in righteousness.

God calls us to name every atrocity, every cruelty, every desecration of life: on all sides. Silence in the face of civilian death isn't neutrality; it's complicity. Christian faith can't be reduced to safe prayers and abstract love. It must take the side of life. It must weep at the grave of every child, whether born in Sderot or Rafah. It must say clearly: stop killing the innocent. Stop justifying the siege. Stop using hostages as leverage. Stop reducing image-bearers to statistics.

Our spirituality teaches us to see rightly. Not as the world sees, but with transfigured eyes. To see every human being (Jewish, Palestinian, Muslim, Christian, Israeli, and Gazan) not as enemy or ally, but as sacred. All are worthy of peace, safety, dignity, and life free from occupation, terror, starvation, or annihilation. The resurrection doesn't erase difference, but it does destroy dehumanization. The empty tomb declares that no person, no people, is disposable.

And so, we speak: for ceasefires that protect civilians, for corridors of compassion, for accountability on every side, for the end of hostage-taking and indiscriminate bombing, for justice that flows not in vengeance but in restoration.

And the church: what of the church?

9

"Let the church be found where the bombs fall, where the mothers grieve, where the hostages wait, and where justice still has a heartbeat."

The church can't afford to be the chaplain of any state or the mouthpiece of any regime. It must be the conscience of the world, bearing witness to a kingdom not built on weapons, fear, or revenge, but on mercy, truth, and reconciliation. Disciples of Jesus must be repairers of breaches, prophets of peace, builders of unlikely tables. Jesus calls us not only to pray for peace, but to make peace: to plead for it, to embody it, to demand it with tears and tenacity.

Let the church be found where the bombs fall, where the mothers grieve, where the hostages wait, and where justice still has a heartbeat. Let us raise our voice, not with partisan anger, but with prophetic courage: crying out for the dignity of all, the liberation of all, and the healing of all.

"The resurrection doesn't erase difference, but it does destroy dehumanization."

Resurrection calls us to embrace the courage to look injustice in the eye and say, "This isn't what love, mercy, righteousness, justice, or shalom looks like." This isn't the world God dreams of. And we won't stop speaking until swords are turned to plowshares, and all dwell secure beneath their own vine and fig tree[6] (dwelling secure in their own apartment and around their family table).

A Way Forward: Presence over Polarity

This isn't a call for political consensus. This is a call for spiritual presence: present enough to grieve on both sides and stubborn enough to refuse demonic binaries. The path the cross teaches is one of reconciliation, justice, peace, and deep prayerfulness. It's salt for wounds, light in darkness, a hand extended not to take sides but to hold them.

---

6 Isaiah 2:4; Micah 4:4

This is what Christian spirituality offers the world today: not a political lobby but an embodied oracle of compassion. Not triumphal slogans, but tear-laden lament. Not dominance, but deep bows.

So, we speak the truth. We name Hamas's evil and Israel's disproportionate fury. No person or group is out of our prayers. And yet our posture remains rooted in resurrection love: that Love made flesh in Jesus Christ, wounded and risen. Divine, cruciform love teaches us that even in the worst war, love can still rise. And so, we must rise with it.

2. I Was a Stranger and You Welcomed Me: Responding to Undocumented Immigrants

The border isn't only a line in the sand or a fence cutting across hills. It's also a place where theology bleeds. It's where fear meets flesh, where the policies of nations touch the skin of people experiencing poverty. Here, humanity is measured in papers, permits, and checkpoints; worth is determined by status; and those who cross without authorization are named "illegal," as if a human life could be outlawed.

But the gospel tells another story.

In the kingdom Jesus proclaimed, there are no outsiders, no disposable lives, no walls that keep grace out. In the kingdom, the stranger isn't a threat but a mirror in which we see our own dependence on mercy. The Scriptures insist that God loves the foreigner and calls the people of God to do the same, not as a political slogan but as a defining mark of holiness.[7] The Incarnation itself is an act of divine crossing: the eternal Word stepping over the border of heaven into the poverty, danger, and fragility of human existence.[8]

If we claim to follow the crucified Christ, our politics, our ethics, and our economics must learn to kneel at this border.

"If we claim to follow the crucified Christ, our politics, our ethics, and our economics must learn to kneel at this border."

---

[7] Deuteronomy 10:18–19; Leviticus 19:33–34.
[8] John 1:14.

The Stranger in the Life of Jesus

Jesus was born under the shadow of empire, to a family on the move. A forced flight to Egypt marked his first days, his parents carrying him across borders as refugees escaping state violence.[9] Before he could walk or speak, Jesus knew the taste of displacement. He knew what it was to live without papers, without power, relying on the mercy of strangers.

Throughout his ministry, Jesus walked along the margins, geographic, social, and moral. He touched lepers no one else would touch, sat with women whose reputations were ruined, dined with tax collectors despised by their own people. He did not simply serve the outsider from a place of safety; he identified with them so deeply that he said, "I was a stranger and you welcomed me."[10] To reject the immigrant, the refugee, the undocumented neighbor, is to turn Christ away at the door.

And the cross? The cross is the ultimate symbol of identification with the powerless, the criminalized, and the condemned. Crucifixion was Rome's way of saying; You have no place here. You have no rights. You don't belong. In Jesus, God absorbed that rejection into the very life of the Trinity. Which means that whenever a human being is rejected at a border, detained in a camp, or deported without mercy, Christ is there, on the wrong side of the wall.

The Kingdom's Reversal of Status

Christian spirituality insists that our identity isn't sealed by the documents we carry but by the image of God we bear. This isn't a pious abstraction. It's a political and spiritual earthquake. It means that the undocumented neighbor is as fully endowed with divine dignity as the citizen, the soldier, or the president. It means that worth can't be earned by assimilation, nor can deportation erase it.

---

[9] Carter, *Matthew and the Margins.*
[10] Matthew 25:35.

Jesus constantly inverted the hierarchy of belonging. "The last will be first," he said, not as poetry but as policy in the kingdom of God.[11] He did not speak of citizenship in terms of passports or visas, but in terms of proximity to the heart of God. In the Beatitudes, it's the poor in spirit, the merciful, the persecuted who are called blessed, not the secure, the credentialed, the protected.

"Our identity isn't sealed by the documents we carry but by the image of God we bear."

This upside-down kingdom calls the church to stand where the world refuses to stand, at the side of the stranger without papers, without advocates, without a voice.

Compassion in a Complicated World

Some will say, it's not that simple. And they're right. Immigration policy is complex. Nations have responsibilities to their citizens. Borders exist in the real world, and governments are responsible for maintaining order and security.

But the call of Christian spirituality isn't to reduce complexity to sentimentality. It's to live as people whose moral compass is set by the cross, not by convenience. The gospel doesn't provide us with a detailed policy platform; it offers us a posture. That posture is shaped by compassion, hospitality, and solidarity, without surrendering truth or discernment.

This means we can acknowledge the need for lawful process while refusing to let legality determine who is worthy of care. It means resisting the temptation to dehumanize those who break immigration laws, recognizing that desperation often drives the risk. It means advocating for systems that are just, merciful, and rooted in the recognition that borders aren't God's ultimate concern; people are.

---

[11] Matthew 20:16.

The Cruciform Lens on State Power

The cross teaches us to be wary of any state that uses power to crush the vulnerable. Rome claimed to be the bringer of order, peace, and prosperity, known as the *Pax Romana*.[12] Yet that peace was enforced by occupation, surveillance, and the execution of those who threatened the imperial narrative. The crucifixion of Jesus unmasks the myth that state violence is ever purely for the common good.

When we see governments detaining children in cages, deporting parents without due process, separating families as a deterrent, or turning away boats of desperate people, the cross teaches us to ask: Who benefits from this cruelty? Whose fears are being fed? Whose humanity is being denied?

"The cross teaches us to be wary of any state that uses power to crush the vulnerable."

Cruciform discipleship calls the church not to be chaplains of border policy but prophets to the nations, reminding them that every person detained, deported, or drowned at sea bears the image of God. A nation's greatness isn't measured by the size of its walls but by the breadth of its welcome.

Hospitality as Resistance

In the ancient world, hospitality wasn't optional; it was a fundamental aspect of social interaction. For Israel, it was a divine command rooted in memory: "You were foreigners in Egypt."[13] For the early church, it was a mark of the Spirit's work, opening homes, tables, and hearts to those who did not belong.[14]

Today, hospitality is an act of resistance against cultures of suspicion. It's a refusal to let fear dictate our ethics. To welcome the

---

12 Wright, *Jesus and the Victory of God.*
13 Leviticus 19:33–34; Deuteronomy 10:19.
14 Pohl, *Making Room.*

undocumented neighbor into our churches, our homes, our schools is to declare that their worth isn't contingent on the approval of the state but on the love of God. It's to live as if the Sermon on the Mount were more binding than immigration law.

Such hospitality isn't naive. It doesn't ignore risk or complexity. It simply refuses to let those realities eclipse obedience to Christ. It trusts that the Spirit can create a table where fear says, "Build a wall."

The Church as Sanctuary

In the tradition of Christian spirituality, the church has often served as a literal sanctuary for those fleeing danger and persecution. Monasteries hid refugees. Cathedrals sheltered the persecuted.[15] Pastors forged safe passage for those hunted by unjust powers.

This legacy isn't nostalgia, it's vocation. In our day, sanctuary might mean providing shelter for those at risk of deportation. It might mean accompanying undocumented neighbors to court hearings. It might mean legal aid, advocacy, and public witness. It might mean risking reputation and resources to embody the love of Christ.

The question isn't whether the church can do these things, but whether it will. Will we be the presence of Christ at the border and in the detention center, or will we remain safe in the suburbs of silence?

Seeing Christ in the Undocumented

Mystical theology insists that Christ hides in the least, the lost, the stranger. "Whatever you did for one of the least of these," Jesus said, "you did for me."[16] This isn't a metaphor. It's a declaration that our treatment of the undocumented is our treatment of Christ.

When we turn away the asylum seeker, we turn away Christ. When we mock the migrant caravan, we mock Christ. When we welcome the stranger, feed the hungry, visit the detainee, we welcome Christ himself.

---

15 Tornkvist, *Sanctuary*.
16 Matthew 25:40.

"Our treatment of the undocumented is our treatment of Christ."

The Cross at the Border

At the border, the logic of the cross collides with the logic of empire. Empire says, protect your own, secure your land, keep out the unworthy. The cross says, lose your life to find it, love your enemy, welcome the stranger.

Empire crucifies the stranger to preserve the illusion of safety. The cross welcomes the stranger even if it costs safety. This isn't recklessness; it's trust in the God who calls us to love beyond borders, even beyond reason.

Advocacy as Spiritual Discipline

Speaking for the undocumented isn't an optional add-on to Christian spirituality; it's integral to our discipleship. Advocacy is a form of prayer with our bodies. It's intercession in public, pleading not only before God but before the rulers of this age.

This may involve writing to lawmakers, participating in peaceful protests, supporting organizations that provide legal aid, or bearing public witness to the humanity of our undocumented neighbors. It means calling out the dehumanizing language that reduces people to "illegals," challenging policies that perpetuate fear, and offering a vision of belonging rooted in the gospel.

The Table of the Lord

Every time we gather at the Lord's Table, we enact the truth that in Christ, there are no outsiders. The Eucharist is borderless. There is one bread, one body, one Spirit. No one is asked for papers at this table. No one is deported from grace.

"No one is asked for papers at this table. No one is deported from grace."

17

Resurrection Beyond the Wall

The hope of the resurrection isn't a sentimental afterthought; it's the engine of Christian courage. Because Christ is risen, we can face the suffering at our borders without despair. We can work for justice even when change feels impossible. We can offer hospitality even when it seems unsafe. We can love beyond the limits of our imagination.

Resurrection assures us that every act of mercy toward the undocumented (every shelter offered, every meal shared, every policy challenged) isn't wasted. It will be gathered into the new creation where every tribe, tongue, and nation will dwell together without fear, without borders, without exile.

Conclusion: Following the Stranger Who Saves

The undocumented immigrant isn't first a problem to be solved but a person to be loved. Their story may be complicated; their legal status may be contested. But their dignity isn't up for debate.

Christian spirituality, shaped by the life, words, and cross of Jesus, calls us to a costly love, a risky hospitality, and a stubborn solidarity. It calls us to stand in the tension of compassion and truth, to seek justice without dehumanizing, and to see in every border crosser the face of Christ.

We follow a Savior who crossed the ultimate border to bring us home. We follow a crucified refugee whose kingdom isn't defended by walls but by wounds. We follow the One who was a stranger, that every stranger might become a friend.

And so, in this age of border walls and detention centers, may the church be known not for the size of its buildings but for the breadth of its welcome. May we be found at the border, bread in hand, arms open, eyes searching for the Christ who still comes to us, without papers, without privilege, but with the power to turn strangers into family.

3. The Wounds That See: Empathy Shaped by the Cross

In some corners of the church, empathy is treated with suspicion. Critics argue that it makes us vulnerable to manipulation or risks replacing truth with sentiment. They say that empathy can slide into permissiveness, blurring moral clarity. Others fear it elevates human feelings above divine revelation.

These cautions aren't trivial. It'd be easy for me to dismiss them out of hand, but I don't want to do that. Empathy untethered from truth can collapse into indulgence. Compassion that never discerns can excuse cruelty. But to dismiss empathy altogether is to miss one of the deepest gifts of Christian spirituality: the invitation to feel with others in a way that mirrors the heart of Christ.

"Christlike empathy isn't sentimentality; it's vision born from the suffering love of Christ."

Christian empathy isn't mere sentimentality. It's the fruit of incarnation. It flows from a God who didn't remain distant but entered flesh and frailty, who bore wounds, hunger, thirst, and rejection. To follow Christ is to enter into this same movement of self-emptying love, to listen with the ears of the heart, and to stand where others stand, not as saviors, but as companions.

"Empathy rooted in Christ isn't weakness. It's cruciform strength: the courage to let another's pain pierce us without rushing to defend ourselves."

The Incarnation as Divine Empathy

The birth of Jesus in a Bethlehem stable wasn't simply a divine strategy for salvation. It was an act of such profound solidarity that it redefined the concept of holiness. The infinite took on the cries of an infant. The One through whom galaxies were formed knew what it was to be hungry, weary, misunderstood, betrayed.

The incarnation is empathy embodied. In Christ, God doesn't look at suffering from afar but steps into the texture of it.[17] This isn't empathy as a technique or mood, but as an ontology: God with us.

When Christians practice empathy, we imitate the God who became touchable. We echo the mystery of Emmanuel. Our willingness to see through another's eyes, to feel the weight of another's burden, isn't a departure from the Gospel but its enactment.

This reshapes our imagination of holiness. Holiness isn't separation from human sorrow but immersion in it. It's compassion that risks contamination, love that breaks down barriers. The God who touched lepers, dined with sinners, and wept at a tomb is the same God who calls disciples to do likewise.

Crucifixion and Wounded Empathy

If the incarnation shows us God's nearness, the crucifixion shows us God's wound. On the cross, Jesus bore more than nails. He bore the derision of empire, the betrayal of friends, the loneliness of abandonment.[18] Here, empathy isn't optional. It's salvific.

The crucifixion reveals the myth that empathy is a sign of weakness. Empathy at the cross is costly. It doesn't avert its gaze from pain. It doesn't shield itself from the anguish of another. It lets the world's grief break the heart.

This is why Christian empathy is different from mere emotional resonance. It isn't about indulging feelings but about standing in

---

[17] Athanasius, *On the Incarnation.*
[18] Moltmann, *The Crucified God.*

solidarity with those who suffer. It shares not only joys but sorrows. It risks not only compassion but cruciform vulnerability.

"The cross teaches us that empathy isn't a skill we deploy but a sacrifice we embody. It costs blood, tears, and presence."

The Resurrection as Redeemed Empathy

If the cross reveals divine solidarity in suffering, the resurrection reveals divine hope in companionship. Empathy doesn't end at the grave. When the risen Christ met Mary Magdalene outside the tomb, when he walked unrecognized with disciples on the road, when he cooked breakfast for weary friends by the sea, he showed that love doesn't abandon.

Resurrection empathy isn't pity. It's presence that breathes new life. It listens to despair yet refuses to concede to it. It looks at the wounds yet proclaims that death doesn't have the last word.

This hope saves empathy from collapsing into despair. To feel deeply without hope is to drown. To feel deeply with resurrection in view is to rise with others, even when the rising is slow, fragile, and hidden.

Mystical Tradition and Empathy

The mystical tradition of the church often speaks of union: union with God, union with others, union with creation. To practice empathy is to live out this union in the ordinary. It's to perceive the image of God shimmering in another, to sense the Spirit groaning with those who groan.

Mystics remind us that empathy begins in silence. Only when we descend into the inner stillness can we hold the cries of others without judgment or defensiveness.[19] Empathy is prayer before it's practice. It's contemplation that opens into communion.

This inner grounding protects empathy from distortion. Without contemplative depth, empathy can become co-dependency or collapse

---

[19] Teresa of Ávila, *The Interior Castle.*

into burnout. But when rooted in the inexhaustible love of Christ, empathy becomes a wellspring that doesn't run dry.

The Prophetic Edge of Empathy

Empathy in Christ isn't passive. It not only sits quietly with the grieving but also rises to confront the forces that cause grief. Genuine empathy fuels justice. To feel the hunger of people experiencing poverty is to demand bread. To feel the fear of the undocumented is to demand safety. To feel the trauma of the oppressed is to cry out for liberation.[20]

This is why some resist empathy: it disrupts comfort. It calls for change. It doesn't allow us to remain neutral. When Jesus wept over Jerusalem, his tears weren't only for personal sorrow but for a city bent on destruction. His lament carried prophetic fire.

"Christlike empathy isn't sentiment that soothes the status quo. It's sanctified sight that exposes injustice, and love that insists on transformation."

The Concerns of Misguided Empathy

But the cautions deserve attention. There's a way of practicing empathy that can lose its way. It can excuse sin by refusing to name it. It can mirror others' feelings so entirely that it abandons discernment. It can become so identified with another that it no longer points to Christ.

Christian spirituality insists that empathy must be yoked to truth. To feel with someone isn't to affirm every choice they make. To sit with another's pain isn't to bless the structures that perpetuate it. The balance is delicate: compassion without compromise, solidarity without surrender.

This balance is possible only because empathy isn't self-generated but Spirit-breathed. It's Christ in us, the hope of glory, who makes us able to bear with one another without being consumed.

---

[20] Gutiérrez, *A Theology of Liberation.*

Responding to the Concerns about Empathy

Some Christians worry that empathy can lead us astray. They fear it might cause us to compromise truth for the sake of compassion, to blur moral boundaries because we've entered too deeply into another's experience. Empathy, they say, risks being guided more by feelings than by faith, more by sentiment than by Scripture. Others worry that carrying the pain of others will overwhelm and exhaust, leaving disciples paralyzed instead of prayerful. Still others suspect that an overemphasis on empathy could shift the focus of the Christian life from obedience to God toward the shifting emotions of human relationships.

These aren't trivial concerns. They arise from a desire to guard faithfulness. They name a real danger: the human heart can be seduced by what feels merciful but may not lead to holiness. Compassion without wisdom can become complicity. A spirituality that listens only to human cries without grounding itself in divine truth risks becoming mired in confusion. To dismiss these cautions outright would be unfaithful to the tradition of discernment that has always been part of Christian spirituality.

When we look at Jesus Christ, we discover empathy as the very path God chose for redemption. The incarnation shows God refusing distance and entering human experience fully and vulnerably. In Christ, divinity bore flesh, walked dusty roads, shared meals, wept at gravesides, and carried betrayal in the body. Empathy here isn't sentimental excess; it's the mystery of incarnation.

The cross intensifies this revelation. At Golgotha, Jesus took the world's suffering into himself. Human pain and violence weren't merely witnessed; they were borne. God didn't suspend judgment nor avoid truth; Christ Jesus fulfilled both as he shouldered sin's consequence in love. Empathy in this light doesn't dilute conviction. It grounds truth more deeply, making it tangible in wounds and mercy. To see through another's eyes is to allow truth to take form in flesh, to breathe through compassion.

The life of Jesus also reveals empathy as a source of power for action. Compassion moved him to heal the sick, feed the hungry, defend the outcast, and confront oppressive powers. Christian empathy, therefore, can't remain passive. It listens deeply, but then it carries bread. It feels the wound, and then it binds. It attends to the cry, and then it steps forward into costly love.

Obedience to Christ makes empathy essential. The command to love God and neighbor demands that we enter the joys and sorrows of others just as Christ entered ours. To carry another's pain is to walk the road Jesus walked, the road of the crucified and risen one who embraced all that is human with redeeming love.

Rooted in the gospel, empathy reveals the holiness of God. It embodies incarnate love where truth and mercy meet. It listens without surrendering discernment, and it acts with a courage that accepts cost. Such empathy, shaped by the cross, doesn't leave us overwhelmed by tears; it immerses us in the living waters of Christ's compassion, from which justice, healing, and hope rise.

Empathy and the Church

In a fragmented world, the church should be the school of empathy. Here, strangers become neighbors, and neighbors become like family.[21] The Eucharist is empathy made sacrament: one bread broken for many, one cup shared among wounds and joys.

Yet too often, the church mirrors the divisions of the world. Empathy shrivels in echo chambers. We learn to feel only for those who look like us, vote like us, and believe like us. But the Spirit is calling the church beyond tribal compassion into cruciform solidarity.

To practice empathy as the body of Christ is to weep with persecuted believers abroad and with victims of racism at home, to rejoice with newly married couples and to ache with those who long for

---

[21] Nouwen, *Life of the Beloved.*

companionship, to sit with the elderly in silence and to sing with the young in joy.

The church without empathy is a clanging cymbal. The church, with empathy, becomes a living body where every member's suffering and joy are shared.

Empathy and Contemporary Issues

Empathy isn't abstract. It touches every public question. To follow Christ in the practice of empathy means:

- We empathize with immigrants and refugees. We seek to understand and respond to the peril of the journey, the ache of displacement, the fear of rejection. We welcome with hospitality, not suspicion.

- We empathize with those experiencing poverty. We seek to understand and respond to the hunger of empty stomachs, the humiliation of exclusion, the fatigue of endless labor. We advocate for justice that provides enough.

- We empathize with the marginalized. We seek to understand and respond to the isolation of those excluded for race, orientation, or status. We stand in solidarity, naming dignity where the world denies it.

- We empathize with the planet itself. We seek to understand and respond to the groaning of creation, the scorching forests, the parched lands, the endangered creatures. We live in ways that heal, not exploit.

- With empathize with those we oppose politically, religiously, or culturally. We seek to understand and respond to what drives their choices, and to hear their stories without caricature. We refuse the temptation of contempt.

This doesn't mean abandoning conviction. It means embodying conviction through compassion. The truth of the Gospel isn't weakened by empathy. It's revealed through it.

Empathy as Cruciform Practice

What, then, does it mean to practice empathy shaped by Christian spirituality?

It means listening before speaking.

It means weeping before judging.

It means standing close enough to be pierced by another's pain.

It means holding stories as sacred, not as arguments to be won.

It means remembering that every person we meet is beloved, bearing the imprint of Christ.

Empathy isn't a technique but a transformation. It's the cruciform life poured into daily encounters. It's the incarnation continued through the body of Christ. It's resurrection hope refusing despair.

"To practice empathy is to live as if the incarnation happened, as if the cross saves, and as if the resurrection opens the tombs of despair."

The Kingdom Shaped by Empathy

Christian nationalism seeks power without compassion. Secular pragmatism seeks results without relationship. Empathy rooted in Christ offers another way: a kingdom where love listens, where presence heals, where wounds aren't hidden but shared.

The church is called to be this kind of community: not sentimental but sacramental, not indulgent but incarnational, not captive to ideologies but shaped by the wounds and wisdom of Jesus.

Empathy in Christ isn't optional. It's discipleship. To refuse empathy is to refuse incarnation. To embrace empathy is to embrace the God who embraced us.

And when the church embodies this, the world will see not just a community that feels, but a kingdom that loves with the very heart of God.

4. Slavery, Freedom, and the Crucified Christ

Some voices today insist that slavery was a long-ago blight with little bearing on our present, even suggesting its impacts are exaggerated. They want us to stop talking about slavery so much and focus on the pleasant parts of our national or collective history. Others unflinchingly confront slavery's brutal legacy and draw lines from past bondage to current injustices like systemic racism, mass incarceration, and human trafficking. Still others feel torn, acknowledging slavery's evils yet uncertain how much the past truly shapes today.

Slavery was unequivocally brutal, dehumanizing, and antithetical to the Gospel of Christ. Its practice treated image-bearing humans as chattel: a grave offense to both neighbor and God. Whatever comforts apologists may claim existed, the reality is that slavery's core was violence and domination, leaving physical and spiritual wounds that echo through generations.

"Slavery was unequivocally brutal, dehumanizing, and antithetical to the gospel of Christ. Its practice treated image-bearing humans as chattel: a grave offense to both neighbor and God."

One stark testimony to slavery's cruelty is the historical image of an enslaved man whose back is crosshatched with keloid scars from repeated whippings.[22] Such barbarity refutes any minimization. Slavery in the United States, for example, meant the routine torture, family

---

22 Equal Justice Initiative, "Racial Justice."

separations, and exploitation of Black men, women, and children. In the British Empire, human beings were treated as property so essential to the economy that upon abolition the government paid millions of pounds: not to the enslaved, but to compensating enslavers for their "loss of property." And in my country, Australia, while chattel slavery wasn't practiced in the same form, Indigenous peoples and indentured Pacific Islanders (victims of "blackbirding" in the 19th century) endured abductions and forced labor that were slavery in all but name. Such facts underscore that the horrors of slavery can't be downplayed.

Any narrative that glosses over chains and whips, auction blocks and stolen children (or the racial caste system these created) is a narrative unmoored from truth. The truthful landscape is sobering: slavery was a "crime against humanity" and a sin against the divine image in every person.[23] It's only by facing this truth that we can hope to heal from its legacy.

Surveying Biblical Perspectives

In the Old Testament (the Hebrew Bible), the defining narrative of Israel is liberation from slavery. For centuries, the Israelites were oppressed as enslaved people in Egypt, suffering under forced labor until God intervened through the Exodus. This foundational event is explicitly woven into Israel's law and memory: "Remember that you were enslaved persons in Egypt and the Lord your God brought you out from there with a mighty hand and an outstretched arm" (Deuteronomy 5:15). Over and over, God's people are commanded to recall their enslaved past. Why? Because memory was meant to cultivate mercy. "Remember you were enslaved persons . . . that is why I command you to do this," says the law, enjoining compassion for the stranger, the servant, the vulnerable. The Israelites knew the heart of an enslaved persons; therefore, they were to write justice and kindness into their society, never

---

[23] The UNESCO Courier, "The Deep Legacy of Slavery"; Pearse, "A Fuller Extract from Gregory of Nyssa on the Evils of Slavery."

forgetting the God who frees the oppressed. Even the Sabbath command in Deuteronomy grounds itself in former slavery: insisting that everyone, servants included, rest on the seventh day, in solidarity with those delivered from bondage. In Israel's laws, fugitive enslaved people weren't to be returned to harsh enslavers, and every seven years, Hebrew bondservants were to be released (and generously provided for) in a mini jubilee of freedom. The Old Testament makes clear that slavery was a grievous reality to be mitigated and remembered, not celebrated. Israel's God identified as "the Lord your God, who brought you out of the land of Egypt, out of the house of slavery": a God on the side of the enslaved.

"Memory was meant to cultivate mercy. 'Remember you were enslaved people . . . that is why I command you to do this,' says the law, enjoining compassion for the stranger, enemy, servant, enslaved person, and vulnerable."

In the New Testament, this liberating thread continues and intensifies. Jesus Christ begins his public ministry by proclaiming release to the captives. In the synagogue at Nazareth, Jesus reads from Isaiah: "The Spirit of the Lord is upon me . . . He has sent me to proclaim liberty to the captives . . . to set free those who are oppressed" (Luke 4:18). Freedom for the oppressed becomes a hallmark of Jesus's mission. Throughout the gospels, we see Jesus uplifting the marginalized and breaking social barriers: befriending tax-enslaved debtors, healing servant-enslaved persons, and treating women and foreigners with a dignity denied by others. He announces a kingdom where the last are first. Yet, we also confront the complex reality that the New Testament was written in a Roman imperial context where slavery was common. Certain epistles (Ephesians, Colossians, 1 Peter) include instructions to enslaved people and enslavers, not because slavery was morally endorsed, but because it was a pervasive social institution of the time. The gospel entered a world "where slavery [was] assumed" as a reality, and the early church had to navigate that reality pastorally.[24] The Apostles urged

---

[24] Grace Communion International, "A Slave as a Brother (Philemon 1–21)."

Christian enslavers and servants to view each other as part of the same redeemed family, even as they awaited the fullness of God's kingdom. The letter to the Ephesians, for instance, tells enslavers to treat their enslaved persons with justice and without threats, "knowing that both of you have the same Master in heaven" (Eph 6:9). Such teaching planted seeds that would, in time, crack the very foundations of slavery. Nowhere is this more evident than in Paul's brief letter to Philemon.

Paul writes on behalf of Onesimus, a fugitive enslaved person transformed by the gospel. Instead of returning Onesimus with condemnation, Paul implores Philemon to receive him "no longer as an enslaved person, but better than an enslaved person: as a dear brother"(Philemon 16). Here, the gospel's radical implications shine through. As some scholars note, Paul's appeal "sowed the seeds of abolition" by urging Christian enslavers to view enslaved people as family in Christ, deserving of freedom.[25] In the community formed by Jesus, the old divisions are fundamentally undermined: "There is neither Jew nor Greek, there is neither enslaved person nor free . . . for you are all one in Christ Jesus" (Galatians 3:28). This was a revolutionary pronouncement in a world stratified by status. The early Christians began addressing each other as adelphoi (brothers and sisters) across lines of class and ethnicity. An enslaved persons like Onesimus could be called "a beloved brother . . . both in the flesh and in the Lord", equal in dignity and honor. Such a vision, fully realized, is utterly incompatible with the institution of slavery. Indeed, even when the New Testament doesn't directly call for slavery's immediate abolition, it sows the seeds of emancipation by asserting the spiritual equality of all people and by inaugurating a community in which enslavers and enslaved people would eat at the same table of fellowship. The gospel message, at its core, is about liberation: not only liberation from sin, but liberation from every yoke that oppresses.

---

[25] Grace Communion International, "A Slave as a Brother (Philemon 1–21)."

Considering Jesus and Slavery

All the promises of Scripture culminate in the person and work of Jesus Christ. To truly understand God's heart on slavery, we turn to Jesus himself: for in him, God personally enters the story of the oppressed. The Incarnation (God becoming human in Jesus) is an astounding act of divine solidarity. The Apostle Paul describes Christ as "emptying himself, taking the form of an enslaved person" (Philippians 2:7). This isn't a mere metaphor; it signals that Jesus didn't come as a worldly king or master, but in humility and lowliness. He was born to a marginal family, in a conquered land, under imperial occupation. From his infancy (fleeing violence as a refugee in Egypt) to his adult ministry associating with people experiencing poverty and exclusion, Jesus fully identified with those at the bottom of social hierarchies. If the worldly powers lorded over enslaved persons, the Lord of heaven chose to become like one. In this, we see God's character: he doesn't endorse human systems of domination but instead joins the oppressed within those systems to redeem them.

Nowhere is this identification clearer than at the Cross. Jesus died the death of an enslaved person; literally. Crucifixion in the Roman Empire was known as "supplicium servile", the punishment reserved for enslaved persons and the lowest of criminals. Roman citizens were usually exempt from the cross; it was deemed too degrading for anyone but enslaved persons, rebels, and the subjugated. Yet Christ "humbled himself and became obedient to the point of death, even death on a cross" (Phil 2:8). In that brutal execution, Jesus aligns himself with all who have been dehumanized and brutalized by oppressive power. He dies a victim of torture and injustice, naked and scorned: the fate of countless enslaved people before and after. By willingly undergoing the "enslaved person's punishment", Jesus exposes the cruelty of our sin and absorbs it into his own body, breaking its hold from the inside out. The Crucifixion is God's great act of "identifying with all the enslaved and degraded," taking their suffering on himself. When we see Christ crucified, we're seeing God in solidarity with the lynched, the whipped, the chained, and the condemned of the world. The One who had the form of God took on the form of an enslaved person, to bring enslaved persons into the form of God's children.

"When we see Christ crucified, we're seeing God in solidarity with the lynched, the whipped, the chained, and the condemned of the world."

And then, resurrection. The resurrection of Jesus is the ultimate act of liberation. On Easter morning, the stone is rolled away, the grave clothes cast off: Christ rises free, never to die again. In this victorious act, every chain (literal or spiritual) is declared breakable. No bondage is final anymore. Death, the last tool of the oppressor, has been defeated. The risen Christ emerges as the Liberator, vindicating all who suffer unjustly. We believe that in rising from the dead, Jesus proved that no chain could hold him, and by extension, no chain can hold forever those who belong to him. As an old hymn rejoices, "He broke the bonds of prison for me." The early church saw the resurrection as a cosmic emancipation proclamation: Christ leading captivity itself captive, throwing open the doors of every metaphorical prison. If the Son sets you free, you are free indeed. Therefore, Christian hope for the enslaved (in the past and present) isn't wishful thinking, but a hope anchored in a historical event. The living Christ calls us to share in his freedom and join his work of setting captives free. In Jesus, God has decisively sided with the oppressed and made a public spectacle of the powers that perpetuate slavery. This is good news: not a partisan talking point or shallow optimism, but a cruciform hope grounded in the God who died an enslaved person's death and rose as the Champion of the oppressed.

In Jesus's life, death, and resurrection, God entered human oppression and broke its ultimate power. The incarnation shows God with us in our lowest state; the Cross shows God for us in sacrificial love; the resurrection shows God victorious for our freedom. For every enslaved person languishing in history's dark corners, for every person today in bondage, Christ's journey from manger to cross to empty tomb shines a light: there is a way out, and God himself walks that path with us.

Viewing Slavery from the Christian Mystical/Spiritual Tradition

Beyond the biblical canon, the Christian mystical and spiritual tradition has long grappled with themes of slavery and freedom: both in the soul and in society. Mystics often spoke of the human person's liberation from the "slavery of sin," using the language of bondage and freedom to describe spiritual growth. But importantly, many carried these metaphors of emancipation into a robust challenge against literal slavery and oppression. They understood that the contemplative vision of God's love has radical social implications: if every person is made one with God, no person can ever truly be owned by another.

Historically, some of the strongest condemnations of slavery came from deeply spiritual thinkers. In the 4th century, St. Gregory of Nyssa (a theologian immersed in mystical reflection on the image of God) preached unequivocally against slaveholding. He asked, "How could anyone who knows the Creator presume to own the image of God?" Gregory thundered at slaveholders: "You condemn people to slavery, when their nature is free . . . You have forgotten the limits of your authority . . . What price did you put on the likeness of God? . . . God wouldn't reduce the human race to slavery, since God, when we had been enslaved to sin, recalled us to freedom".[26] His words ring across the centuries as a mystical indictment of slavery's arrogance. To possess a human being, Gregory argues, is delusional folly: an insult to God who made each person for communion with Godself. The closer one draws to God, the more "the logic of ownership" shatters: you realize that each neighbor is sacred, not property.

"The closer one draws to God, the more the logic of ownership shatters: you realize that each neighbor is sacred, not property."

---

[26] Pearse, "A Fuller Extract from Gregory of Nyssa on the Evils of Slavery."

This same spiritual clarity animated later abolitionist voices, many of whom were people of profound faith. Sojourner Truth, for example, was a Black woman born into slavery in New York who became a fiery preacher, abolitionist, and mystic. After gaining her freedom, she sensed a divine call to itinerant ministry, even changing her name to reflect that call. "When I left the house of bondage," she said, "I wasn't going to keep nothing of Egypt on me. So, I went to the Lord and asked him to give me a new name . . . And the Lord gave me Truth, because I was to declare the truth to the people".[27] Rooted in biblical imagination, Sojourner Truth cast her own emancipation as an Exodus from "Egypt" and understood her mission as prophetically speaking truth to a nation still in sin. She and other formerly enslaved Christians, like Frederick Douglass, exposed the hypocrisy of a slaveholding society claiming to be Christian. Douglass famously wrote that he loved the "pure, peaceable, and impartial Christianity of Christ" too much to confuse it with "the corrupt, slaveholding . . . Christianity of this land", declaring one must be enemy to the other.[28] His profound spirituality (honed through suffering and sustained by prayer) gave him eyes to see that any religion which enshrined slavery was a sham, "the boldest of all frauds".[29] True faith, for Douglass, aligned with the liberating Christ, not the oppressor's whip.

From Catholic monks opposing the enslaved person trade, to Quaker contemplatives quietly boycotting enslaved person-produced goods, to liberation theologians in Latin America calling the oppressed "the crucified people": the mystical stream within Christianity has consistently nurtured empathy for the enslaved and a cry for justice. These spiritual teachers understood that loving God and loving one's neighbor are inseparable. If, in prayer, one experiences union with a God whose Spirit "groans" with the oppressed (Romans 8:26), one can't remain silent about human bondage. The likes of Sojourner Truth,

---

[27] Vicari, "7 Sojourner Truth Quotes on Equality Grounded in Faith."
[28] Robert's Blog, "Two Frederick Douglass Quotes."
[29] Robert's Blog, "Two Frederick Douglass Quotes."

Frederick Douglass, and Harriet Tubman (who led enslaved persons to freedom by relying on God's guidance), as well as countless unnamed enslaved persons who sang spirituals of deliverance, all demonstrate an "abolitionist spirituality." Their faith fueled their resistance. They carried within them a mystical vision of a just world born from the heart of God. In that vision, each human being is an icon of divine glory, and it's unthinkable that an icon of God could ever be mere property. As we drink from this rich spiritual well, we too are invited to see with transfigured eyes: the face of Christ in the enslaved, and the face of the enslaved in Christ. This contemplative seeing empowers us to proclaim, with the mystics, that slavery has no place in God's plan for humanity.

Addressing Modern Slavery

It's tempting to consign slavery to the past (to ancient empires or 18th-19th century plantations), but slavery didn't end with legal abolition; it merely assumed new forms. In truth, modern slavery is alive and among us, though it often hides in the shadows. By modern slavery, we mean practices like human trafficking, forced labor, debt bondage, forced prostitution, child soldiering, forced marriage, and other forms of extreme exploitation wherein people are controlled and treated as property. Shockingly, on any given day in 2021, an estimated 50 million people were living in modern slavery around the world.[30] This includes about 28 million in forced labor (working in fields, factories, fishing boats, or domestic servitude under coercion) and some 22 million in forced marriages, often essentially sold as chattel.[31] These aren't mere statistics but lives: the girl trafficked for sex in a city not far from here; the migrant laborer trapped under threat on a foreign worksite; the boy forced to mine minerals that end up in our smartphones. Slavery today ensnares people of every race and nation, though it disproportionately affects the poorest and those marginalized by prejudice (such as ethnic

---

30 International Labour Organization, "50 Million People in Modern Slavery."
31 International Labour Organization, "50 Million People in Modern Slavery."

minorities and lower castes). We must open our eyes to the continuity: the same evil that whipped backs on a plantation now works children in sweatshops or coerces runaways in brothels. The tools of terror and dehumanization have changed little: only the circumstances.

Furthermore, the legacy of historical slavery continues to shape systemic injustices, particularly in countries like the United States and Australia. In the U.S., the racist ideology invented to justify African chattel slavery (the "belief that nonwhite people are less human than white people") didn't vanish after abolition.[32] It morphed into Jim Crow segregation, and today its vestiges remain in what many term the new Jim Crow: mass incarceration and persistent racial inequity. The 13th Amendment to the U.S. Constitution outlawed slavery "except as punishment for crime," and almost immediately, Southern states exploited that exception, arresting Black citizens en masse for petty "crimes" to lease them as convict labor. As one modern prisoner-rights activist wrote, "Slavery never ended in this country . . . [after 1865] anybody convicted of a crime could be leased out by the state to private corporations . . . In some ways that created worse conditions than under slavery".[33] To this day, tens of thousands of American inmates (disproportionately people of color) perform arduous labor for pennies, and refusal can land them in solitary confinement.[34] Many have called this "prison labor . . . modern slavery", an echo of the past on today's chain gangs.[35] More broadly, the wealth gap, health disparities, and over-policing experienced by Black communities are traceable to centuries of slavery and racist policy that followed. The myth of racial hierarchy born in slavery "survived [slavery's] abolition . . . and spawned our mass incarceration crisis", as the Equal Justice Initiative observes.[36] The

---

[32] Equal Justice Initiative, "Racial Justice."

[33] Johnson, "Prison Labor Is Modern Slavery. I've Been Sent to Solitary for Speaking Out."

[34] Johnson, "Prison Labor Is Modern Slavery. I've Been Sent to Solitary for Speaking Out."

[35] Johnson, "Prison Labor Is Modern Slavery. I've Been Sent to Solitary for Speaking Out."

[36] Equal Justice Initiative, "Racial Justice."

United Kingdom, too, faces calls to confront how the profits of the transatlantic enslaved person trade seeded its national wealth, and how colonial-era attitudes linger. In Australia, the oppression of Indigenous peoples (though different in form from Atlantic slavery) shares the dynamic of dehumanization and exploitation. Aboriginal and Torres Strait Islander peoples were often forced to work for little or no pay well into the 20th century (a practice now referred to as "stolen wages"). Indigenous children were forcibly removed from families in the abusive assimilative policies of the Stolen Generations. And today, Aboriginal and Torres Strait Islander peoples are grossly overrepresented in prisons, a result of intergenerational trauma and systemic bias. In all these cases, we see that the evil root of slavery (the reduction of persons to less-than-human status for others' gain) still bears fruit in our world.

Yet the very same biblical and spiritual vision that compelled us to reject old chattel slavery also calls us to confront these present forms of bondage. We're heirs of a faith that proclaims liberation to captives; we can't be content while people are trafficked in our cities or trapped in forced labor abroad, producing the goods we consume. We worship a God who hears the cry of the oppressed; we must ask whose cries we have yet to hear today. The continuity of slavery's effects imposes a continuity of responsibility: to finish the unfinished work of emancipation in every realm. This means advocating for justice in policies: from anti-trafficking laws and corporate supply-chain accountability (ensuring products are free of forced labor) to prison reforms that restore dignity. It means addressing the "weight of this legacy" of enslavement in how we treat racial minorities and migrants.[37] It means educating ourselves and others, so that, as UNESCO urges, "we take into account the weight of this legacy . . . to build a more inclusive world".[38] Above all, it means recognizing in each suffering neighbor the face of Christ and responding with the love and urgency that such

---

[37] The UNESCO Courier, "The Deep Legacy of Slavery."
[38] The UNESCO Courier, "The Deep Legacy of Slavery."

recognition demands. Slavery in any guise is antithetical to the gospel; therefore, the gospel compels us to action until all God's children are free.

Wrestling With Contemporary Debates About Slavery

There are movements today that seek to soften or relativize the history of slavery. In textbooks and public debates, we sometimes hear it described as a regrettable but overstated practice, one among many injustices of the past, or even as an institution that wasn't "so bad" for those forced into it. Others admit its brutality but insist it's time to "move on" and stop tracing present injustices to that legacy. These perspectives often emerge from fatigue, denial, or fear (fear of blame, shame, or what an honest reckoning might demand).

But minimizing slavery isn't simply a political or historical error; it's a profound spiritual distortion. It ignores the witness of those who bore scars on their backs and grief in their souls. It overlooks the clear biblical mandate to remember. "Remember that you were enslaved people in Egypt," says Deuteronomy, "and the Lord your God brought you out"(Deut 5:15). Forgetfulness was the enemy of justice for Israel, because forgetting leads to repetition. To deliberately diminish the horror of slavery is to repeat the sin of Pharaoh: hardening our hearts against the cries of the oppressed.

Minimization is also wrong because it insults the gospel. Jesus proclaimed freedom for the captives, and he identified himself with the condemned and crucified. To suggest that slavery was somehow tolerable is to suggest that chains don't matter, that degradation is survivable, and that God doesn't take sides with the enslaved. Yet the cross shows the opposite: God so identifies with those cast aside that God chose the punishment of enslaved people as the place to reveal divine love.

"To minimize slavery is to forget, and to forget is to betray both the oppressed and the God who sets them free."

From the mystical and spiritual tradition, we learn that every human being bears the image of God, and to own another person is to desecrate that image. To dismiss slavery as overstated is, in effect, to say that desecrating God's image was a minor offense. Voices like Gregory of Nyssa, Sojourner Truth, and Frederick Douglass expose that as blasphemy. They remind us that the Spirit cries out wherever human beings are reduced to property. To ignore or diminish those cries today is to resist the Spirit's groaning.

Finally, minimization ignores the continuity between past and present. The wounds of slavery didn't disappear with abolition. They hardened into structures, ideologies, and inequities that still shape societies today: systemic racism, mass incarceration, Indigenous dispossession, and global human trafficking. To say "it wasn't so bad" or "it's over now" is to cover wounds without healing them. True healing requires truth-telling, lament, repentance, and repair.

The church, then, must be a community that refuses minimization. We're a people of memory. We tell the story of a crucified Savior at every Eucharist. We remember Israel's slavery at every Passover. We remember because remembering redeems. Forgetting perpetuates bondage; remembrance opens the way to freedom. To minimize slavery is to forget, and to forget is to betray both the oppressed and the God who sets them free.

Embracing a Prophetic and Pastoral Posture

How should we as people of faith respond, in heart and deed, to the grievous reality of slavery past and present? We're called to adopt both a prophetic and pastoral posture, grounded in the Holy Spirit: even a mystical posture of prayerful solidarity.

Prophetically, we must speak and act with unflinching truth-telling about the horror and sin of slavery. The Old Testament prophets, when confronted with oppression, raised their voices like trumpets. Likewise, the church must not shy away from naming slavery (and the racism and exploitation that flow from it) as a grave evil that offends God. This means rejecting the minimization or denialism that is present among us. It means, for example, correcting narratives that the enslaved were "well treated" or that we should "stop dwelling on the past." We answer such claims not with political vitriol, but with the firm authority of truth and love. In love, we warn that oppressing or ignoring the oppressed brings God's judgment. As people of the Word, we recall that 1 Timothy 1:10 explicitly lists "enslavers" (enslaved person-traders) among the ungodly. We align with figures like William Wilberforce and the abolitionists who "denounced slavery as inconsistent with the spirit of the gospel".[39] A prophetic stance today may involve advocacy: supporting reparative measures for historical injustices, challenging racist structures, and demanding more decisive action against human trafficking rings. It's holy anger on behalf of the powerless, and holy courage to face uncomfortable truths. In this posture, we echo the biblical prophets: "Let justice roll down like waters, and righteousness like an ever-flowing stream"(Amos 5:24). We call the world (and the church itself, wherever it has been complicit) to confession and repentance. Like the prophet Daniel confessing the sins of his nation, we too lament our history: "We have sinned and done wrong." Such prophetic lament is the beginning of healing.

Yet even as we cry out against injustice, we do so with a pastoral heart. A pastoral posture means we not only denounce evil but also nurture and guide God's people toward healing and action. We acknowledge that confronting slavery's legacy can stir defensiveness, guilt, or despair. A pastoral approach meets people where they are and invites them into a journey of empathy and growth. We encourage our communities to lament: to grieve with those who grieve, weeping over the wounds that slavery inflicted on generations. There's profound power in shared lamentation: it breaks the heart of stone and opens us to compassion. In worship, this might mean observing a day of remembrance for victims of slavery and trafficking, allowing stories of

---

[39] Anyabwile, "Doug Wilson's Views on Race, Racism, Slavery and the Bible."

the enslaved to be heard, their names honored. Pastorally, we also lead in confession and repentance. The church can create safe spaces for people (especially those from privileged groups) to lay down defensiveness and honestly confess how we have benefited from or been indifferent to systems built on slavery. Repentance isn't about wallowing in guilt; it's about turning and doing right. Thus, we guide repentant hearts into concrete acts of change. This could be as personal as befriending and mentoring a survivor of trafficking in your city, or as communal as rallying a congregation to support anti-slavery organizations. It might involve examining our own consumer choices (are we inadvertently funding forced labor?) and making more just decisions. The pastoral stance also emphasizes hospitality to survivors of modern slavery. "Pastoral" literally relates to shepherding; we're called to gently tend those who have been through the valley of the shadow of death. Churches can partner in providing safe houses, job training, or simply a loving spiritual family for people coming out of trafficking or exploitation. In doing so, we live out Isaiah's call to "bind up the brokenhearted" and set captives on the road to wholeness.

Finally, a mystical or contemplative posture undergirds both the prophetic and pastoral. St. Paul reminds us that "the Spirit intercedes with sighs too deep for words" (Rom 8:26): the Spirit groans along with creation's suffering. When we join our prayer with the oppressed, our very groaning becomes prayer. To sit in silence before God, holding the pain of enslaved peoples in our hearts, isn't a passive act. It's deeply spiritual resistance. The mystics tell us that God is especially present in the distressing disguise of the poor and captive. So, when we prayerfully stand in solidarity (when we, for instance, participate in a prayer vigil for trafficking victims, or incorporate prayers of lament and hope regarding slavery's legacy in our liturgy), we're mystically joining the Spirit's own lament. This sustains us. We don't fight these giant evils by our strength alone, but by the Spirit of the Lord, who anoints us to bring good news to the poor and freedom to the oppressed. A cruciform life (shaped by the cross) will involve both carrying the cross (entering the pain of others

41

through empathy) and pointing to the empty tomb (holding out hope). Our posture, then, is one of humility and hope, anger and compassion, action and prayer: all held together by the love of Christ.

Living Out Cruciform Hope

We end not in despair or paralysis, but in hope: specifically, cruciform hope shaped by the death and resurrection of Jesus. After confronting the grim truths of slavery and its aftermath, one might feel overwhelmed or guilt-ridden. But the Christian story never ends at Golgotha; it proceeds to Easter. Cruciform hope means that, through the Cross, new life is possible even in the bleakest situations. It's a hope that has been refined by suffering, a hope with nail scars, yet an unbreakable hope.

What does this hope look like in the context of slavery? It looks like the certainty that evil doesn't have the final word. The same Christ who declared on the cross, "It's finished," is now risen and declaring, "Behold, I make all things new." We hold fast to the promise that Christ "sets the captives free" and "breaks every chain." We have seen this promise partially fulfilled in history: the abolition of legal slavery in many nations was nothing short of a moral miracle brought about by courageous faith and struggle. If such a change were possible, then greater change is possible now and in the future. Our hope isn't a naive wish that "someone" will fix these problems, but an active trust that Jesus is already at work setting captives free and calls us to co-labor with him. Every time a trafficking victim is rescued and starts a new life, every time a prejudice is overcome and a former enemy is embraced as a brother, every time a person chooses reconciliation over bitterness, the resurrection is breaking through. We see signs of this hope in survivors who, against all odds, heal and even help others heal; in multi-ethnic congregations that stand together as a testimony to the fact that, in Christ, enslaved and free persons are truly one; in young people educated about justice who feel called to be modern-day abolitionists. These are the firstfruits of the kingdom.[40]

Even as we labor in hope, we remember that ultimate liberation is God's work. Christian hope is cruciform precisely because it acknowledges the pain (the cross) even as it anticipates the victory (the resurrection). We don't paper over the wounds of history; we touch them, like Thomas touching Christ's scars, and thereby come to deeper faith. We lament, we repent, we strive, and we also rejoice, because we know how the story ends. The biblical vision of the end of days is profoundly egalitarian and free: "a great multitude . . . from every nation and tribe and people and language" gathered in praise (Revelation 7:9), former oppressors and the oppressed reconciled by the Lamb of God. In that heavenly city, no captive walks in chains and no person calls another "master" except God alone. "In heaven, Black and White are one in the love of Jesus," as Sojourner Truth said, "and if white people want to find themselves in heaven, they must go without their prejudice".[41] Our task now is to embody that liberated future here on earth, as much as possible, through the Spirit's power.

"Christ has died (entering our bondage); Christ is risen (shattering our chains); Christ will come again (completing our liberation). In that promise, we work and we watch (with gravity, with compassion, and with unyielding hope) until every enslaved person is free."

So, we conclude with hope: a grounded, cruciform hope. We believe every act of justice, every soul set free, every ounce of reconciliation is participation in Christ's triumph. We don't journey in vain. As Dr. Martin Luther King Jr. (one of the great modern prophets) often reminded us, "The arc of the moral universe is long, but it bends toward justice." We can say this because we trust the hands doing the bending: nail-scarred hands that hold the keys of death and hell.

---

[40] Vicari, "7 Sojourner Truth Quotes on Equality Grounded in Faith."
[41] Vicari, "7 Sojourner Truth Quotes on Equality Grounded in Faith."

Therefore, we don't lose heart. The legacy of slavery is long and heavy, yes, but the mercy and might of God are longer and stronger. The same Jesus who wept at Lazarus's tomb (entering our sorrow) also shouted "Lazarus, come forth!" (overcoming death itself). He weeps with those still oppressed, and he calls us to help "unbind them and let them go." And one day, when all is fulfilled, we will celebrate in the fullness of freedom together: formerly enslaved and formerly enslaver, both redeemed by grace, singing the song of Moses and the Lamb: "Free at last, free at last; thank God Almighty, we're free at last."

This is the cruciform hope we cling to and proclaim. Christ has died (entering our bondage); Christ is risen (shattering our chains); Christ will come again (completing our liberation). In that promise, we work and we watch (with gravity, with compassion, and with unyielding hope) until every enslaved person is free.

PART II—MISSION BEYOND EMPIRE: GLOBAL CHRISTIANITY AND THE NEW IMAGINATION

Part 2 charts a vision of mission and faith that resists colonial residues, honors global diversity, and recognizes the Spirit's movement beyond Western centers.

5. What is Christian Mission?

It feels like everyone in Christianity is talking about mission these days. Mission has been a buzzword for decades, likely because Christians are wrestling to make sense of their role in changing societies and are often passionate about being faithful to God's mission in the world.

David Bosch once famously wrote, "Mission refers to a permanent and intrinsic dimension of the church's life. The church "is missionary by its nature" . . . and it's impossible to talk about church without at the same time talking about mission. Because God is a missionary God, God's people are missionary people. The church's mission isn't secondary to its being; the church exists in being sent and in building up itself for its mission . . . Ecclesiology doesn't precede missiology; there can't be church without an intrinsic missionary dimension. And Shenk (1991:107) quotes Emil Brunner's famous adage: "The church exists by mission, just as fire exists by burning."[42]

Mission is Often a Vague Word

The word "mission" has been widely used in recent decades, but its meaning is often vague and elusive. "Mission" seems to be a word that can mean whatever the speaker or writer wants it to mean, so it's not clear people are always talking about the same thing. We end up with vague ideas about mission that adapt to the ideologies, theologies, tastes, and preferences of those discussing mission. Perhaps few words are more widely used in Christianity today than "mission," yet the word's

---

[42] Bosch, *Believing in the Future*, 32.

meaning is vague and elusive and malleable to the theologies and ideologies of those who use it.

This is why I love the missiology of David Bosch and Christopher Wright; because they ground their theologies of mission in the grand narrative of the Bible (Genesis through Revelation), preventing their theologies and practices of mission from being a mere extension of their egos, tastes, and personal preferences.

My Definition of Mission

Here's my condensed, one-sentence definition of Christian mission, which emerges from my examination of the Bible:

"Mission is joining God's redemptive and restorative work through Jesus Christ, proclaiming the gospel, making disciples, and embodying Christ's love, justice, and reconciliation in the power of the Spirit among all peoples and creation."

Mission is notoriously difficult to define. So, in addition to that one-sentence definition, I'll also offer a more comprehensive definition. What follows is a long definition, as I try to do justice to the marvelous portrait of mission in the entire Bible:

"Christian mission is joining God's work in redeeming and restoring all humanity and creation through Jesus Christ. In the grand narrative of the Bible (Genesis through Revelation), we see that God is a missionary God who invites us to join in the divine mission to save humanity from sin and death and to restore all creation to God's original good and perfect intent.

"Mission is integral (holistic), integrating word, sign, and deed. Mission is doing the work of Jesus Christ in the power of the Spirit: proclaiming the gospel, making disciples, moving in the power and love of the Spirit, pursuing justice, embodying reconciliation and peacemaking, serving others, embodying Christ through our presence, building communities of believers, caring for creation, suffering for righteousness, living out Christ's teachings, relying on prayer and God's guidance, and loving God, neighbors, strangers, and enemies. We're God's sent people who go with the Good News of salvation and restoration in Christ Jesus, proclaiming the gospel, incarnating the gospel among neighbors and cultures, and making disciples of Jesus Christ among all peoples and nations: these disciples also go and make more disciples.

"Mission is from everywhere to everywhere, and from everyone to everywhere: so, it must be polyvocal, polycentric, and intercultural. Mission is joining Jesus Christ in the power of the Spirit and the gospel, as Christ transforms people and societies and reveals God's kingdom."

6. Shaping Christian Spirituality and Theology for a New Urban World

"To take head on oppressive structures like consumerism, technology, militarism, multinational capitalism, international communism, racism, and sexism, we need a spirituality of missional engagement . . . Mission without spirituality can't survive any more than combustion without oxygen." *Orlando E. Costas*

"A xeroxed copy of a theology made in Europe or North America can never satisfy the theological needs of the Church in the Third World. Now that the Church has become a world community, the time has come for it to manifest the universality of the Gospel in terms of a theology that isn't bound by a particular culture but shows the many-sided wisdom of God." *C. René Padilla*

The world is rapidly urbanizing. Urban theology, spirituality, and mission are deeply connected. Urban missionaries need to cultivate robust expressions of urban theology and spirituality.

In 2014, an International Society for Urban Mission (ISUM) Summit Working Group on "Spirituality and Theology for a New Urban World" spent a few days considering this issue. There were twenty-six participants in that ISUM Working Group. Our conversations were an expression of *glocalisation*. Local stories and global themes enriched each other. Applying processes of Appreciative Inquiry and World Café, this ISUM Working Group explored the shape of "spirituality and theology for a new urban world". And we did this through conversations, storytelling, prayer, immersion experiences, meals, tears, and laughter.

We also formulated a "call to action" for the broader church. A new urban world demands new forms of urban Christian spirituality and theology.

Glocal Conversations in a New Urban World

Urban theology, spirituality, and mission are deeply connected. Urban missionaries need to cultivate robust expressions of urban theology and spirituality. Orlando E. Costas and C. René Padilla are right. "We need a spirituality of missional engagement." And we need a global theology that "shows the many-sided wisdom of God".

The International Society for Urban Mission held a summit on *Signs of Hope in the City*, in Kuala Lumpur, Malaysia, in 2014. This summit was a partnership among ISUM, Urban Neighbours of Hope (UNOH), the Micah Network, and the World Evangelical Alliance's (WEA) Theological Commission. It involved "interactive, participatory, hands-on, immersion opportunities, keynotes, lecturers, and workshops". Participants came from all over the globe. A few hundred Majority World, indigenous, First Nations, and Western thinkers and activists came together for those days. They explored the theology and practices of integral, transformational, and urban mission. And, together, they looked for "signs of hope in the city". They identified places where God is at work bringing hope, healing, reconciliation, life, and transformation.

Majority World and Western leaders participated in discussion, prayer, integral mission, and ISUM Working Groups. The goal was to grapple with key issues and ask key questions. How do we recruit, equip, and sustain urban mission today? How do we release church movements among the urban poor? How can we immerse ourselves in and transform urban neighbourhoods? How do we empower urban children and young people? How does the church serve and liberate the oppressed—and others suffering from urban injustice? What needs to happen for poorer urban centers to develop economically, socially, and spiritually? How do we join God in the challenges and opportunities of multi-faith cities?

The Summit was a thrilling example of how Majority World, indigenous, First Nations, and Western leaders can cooperate. It was a time to come together in an environment of mutual learning and enrichment; a window into how local contexts and global themes can enrich each other. This emerged from ISUM's commitment to "solidarity, fellowship, and insight between urban Christian leaders in the Western and Majority Worlds".

Majority World, indigenous, and Western leaders, thinkers, and churches can stretch and enrich each other. But they need to be open and attentive to each other. They need learning postures and open hearts and minds. And passion for learning and collaboration, and for Jesus and his kingdom. And their vision and values must align with those of the kingdom of God.

The global church needs global theologies. And it needs local theologies. Local and global theologies are both necessary if we're to shape theological reflections that are adequate for a globalized world.

The church needs theologies that are ready for the emerging shape of Christian spirituality and mission in a new urban world.

Harold A. Netland defines globalized theology this way: "Globalizing theology is theological reflection rooted in God's self-revelation in Scripture and informed by the historical legacy of the Christian community through the ages, the current realities in the world, and the diverse perspectives of Christian communities throughout the world, with a view to greater holiness in living and faithfulness in fulfilling God's mission in all the world through the church. Thus, theology is to be an ongoing process in which Christian communities throughout the world participate."[43]

This definition is helpful. The church needs both a globalized and *globalized* theology. A *glocal* theology happens when local voices engage global conversations. And it's a theology rooted in spirituality and mission.

---

[43] Ott and Netland, *Globalizing Theology*, 30.

What do I mean by *glocal*? The local (the local, contextual, homogeneous) and the global (the global, universal, heterogeneous) interconnect. Our globalized world has blurred the boundaries between the local and the global. The local is a dimension of the global. The global shapes the local. The two are interdependent. They enable each other. They form each other, reciprocally. While tensions exist, the global and local aren't opposing forces. They connect—deeply and inextricably. "Not only are the global and the local inseparably intertwined; they also determine each other's respective forms. From a sociological perspective, the glocalisation means generally the organic and symbiotic relationship between the global and the local."[44]

All local Christian theologies and spiritualities can contribute to *glocal* conversations. We need Western, indigenous, First Nations, and Majority World voices. Local and global conversations must meet and enrich each other in constructive ways. When they do, we end up with worthwhile *globalized* theologies and practices. I believe that we must develop urban missions through glocal conversations. *Glocalisation* can help us apply urban theology in the concrete practices of urban mission and spirituality. Worthwhile *glocalisation* is about dialogue, learning, and partnership. It's about the courage to listen to others, and venture into the unknown.

This is what the 2014 ISUM Summit in Malaysia was all about. Local and global conversations enriched each other. And this resulted in enriched urban missions, theologies, and spiritualities. Christians from all over the world came together at this Summit. They listened, conversed, and learned from each other. And they formed partnerships in urban mission. What a thrill and a privilege!

René August and I (Graham Hill) had the privilege of co-facilitating an ISUM Working Group at the 2014 ISUM Summit in Kuala Lumpur. The Work Group was on "Spirituality and Theology for a New Urban World". There were twenty-six participants in that ISUM

---

[44] Tizon, *Transformation after Lausanne*, 207.

Working Group. Our conversations were an expression of *glocalisation*. Local stories and global themes enriched each other. This happened through prayerful conversation. Working Group participants came from all over the globe. Together, we explored the shape of "spirituality and theology for a new urban world". And we did this through conversations, storytelling, prayer, immersion experiences, meals, tears, and laughter. This paper summarizes our discoveries and learnings.

Processes of Discernment

With the theme, "Christian Spirituality and Theology for a New Urban Context", the twenty-six participants in our ISUM Working Group agreed to discern important themes in urban spirituality and theology through two group processes: (1) Appreciative Inquiry, and (2) World Café. We integrated these two group processes. And we sought to hear what the Spirit was saying to us about urban spirituality and theology in our conversations, ministries, contexts, immersion experiences, and prayers.

1. First Discernment Process: Appreciative Inquiry

The first process our ISUM Working Group applied was Appreciative Inquiry. Appreciative Inquiry is a popular method for group discernment and leading organizational change. The Spirit of Christ is at work in almost every setting. This means that we can discern the positive, life-giving, and transformational activity of the Spirit in almost every setting. We only need eyes to see. We need to learn to "appreciate" where God is at work and what he is doing. As we reflect on our ministries, contexts, conversations, and immersion experiences, we appreciate what God is doing and what he is saying to us.

"Appreciative" here means, "to value what is best about a human system… To deliberately notice, anticipate, and heighten the positive potential… To see beyond obstacles, problems, and limitations, and to generate hope in the human capacity to achieve potential.... [Appreciation is] the art of valuing those factors that give life."[45]

Building on the work of Jane Watkins, Bernard Mohr, and others, Mark Lau Branson says that Appreciative Inquiry has five generic processes. (1) Choose the positive as the focus of inquiry. (Affirmative topic choice). (2) Inquire into stories of life-giving forces. (*Discovery*—"appreciate what is"). (3) Locate themes that appear in the stories. Then, select topics for further inquiry. (*Dream*—"imagine what might be"). (4) Create shared images for a preferred future. (*Design*—"determine what should be"). (5) Find innovative ways to create that future. (*Destiny*—"create what will be").[46]

Jane Watkins and Bernard Mohr write the following about these five processes: "The limitations of the written word impose certain constraints on our description of the generic processes. For ease of comprehension, we have listed them above in sequence. But... the generic processes don't begin and end neatly. They overlap and repeat themselves without predictability, which is another reason that you must be grounded in the theory, research, and principles of AI as you begin translating these generic processes into practice."[47]

Mark Lau Branson describes the value of Appreciative Inquiry this way: "Leadership... is about creating spaces and environments in which the people of God can discern God's presence and initiatives in their lives, among their neighbors, and in their contexts. This isn't the work of experts but rather a way of life among the everyday people in our churches. Keys to this work include how we ask questions, receive and interpret the stories and perspectives we hear, and then shape experiments for next steps... The thesis of Appreciative Inquiry is that an organization, such as a church, can be recreated by its conversations. And if that new creation is to feature the most life-giving forces and

---

[45] Barrett, "Organizational Dynamics," 10.
[46] Lau Branson, *Memories, Hopes, and Conversations*, 28–29.
[47] Watkins and Mohr, *Appreciative Inquiry*, 40.

forms possible, then the conversations must be shaped by appreciative questions."[48]

2. Second Discernment Process: World Café

The second process our ISUM Working Group applied was World Café. We found World Café a helpful overlay upon Appreciate Inquiry. It enhanced conversations, hospitality, questioning, contribution, cross-pollination, and harvesting collective discoveries. Juanita Brown and David Isaacs describe the seven principles of World Café as:

1. *Set the context.* Clarify the purpose and parameters of the conversation and its place in the larger environment in which it will happen.

2. *Create hospitable space.* Provide a welcoming, safe, life-serving environment.

3. *Explore questions that matter.* Invite collective attention into what's important to the participants.

4. *Encourage everyone's contribution.* Engage meaningful participation by each person, with real respect.

5. *Cross-pollinate and connect diverse perspectives.* Facilitate juicy diversity and equally juicy interconnectedness.

6. *Listen together for patterns, insights, and deeper questions.* Help coherent group insight emerge naturally from the dance of individual perspectives and passions.

7. *Harvest and share collective discoveries.* Make the group's collective intelligence visible to itself.[49]

3. Integrating Appreciate Inquiry and World Café

Our 2014 ISUM Working Group on "spirituality and theology for a new urban world" sought to integrate the two processes of Appreciative Inquiry and World Café. Combined, Appreciate Inquiry and World Café

---

[48] Branson, *Memories, Hopes, and Conversations*, xiii.
[49] Brown and Isaacs, *The World Café.*

offered our ISUM Working Group a process for discerning emerging themes in urban spirituality and theology.

Here's the process that unfolded. We followed these steps as an ISUM Working Group:

1. *We identified carriers of hope.* (We recognized stories from our lives, contexts, urban missions, and immersion experiences that show us where God is working to form fresh approaches to urban spirituality and theology. These are stories that give us insight and fill us with hope.).

2. *We identified challenges to hope.* (We detected things that dampen or extinguish such hope.).

3. *We identified questions that emerge.* (We named questions about urban Christian spirituality and theology that emerge from these stories of hope and challenges to hope.).

4. *We celebrated being Christians in an urban and diverse context.* (We asked, "What do we celebrate about doing spirituality and theology in an *urban* context?" And "What do we celebrate about doing spirituality and theology in a *diverse* context?").

5. *We connected urban theology and urban spirituality.* (We investigated the practical connections between urban theology and urban spirituality, witness, life, and service.).

6. *We identified new practices and habits.* (At the end of the process, we discussed how we might form new practices and habits that enhance urban spirituality and theology. We also considered lifestyle issues and developing resources. We considered the shape of a "call to action". This included recommendations to the broader church).

I describe some of our findings in the rest of this paper.

Carriers of Hope

Many of the twenty-six people in our ISUM Summit Working Group on "Spirituality and Theology for a New Urban World" are serving among the urban poor. So, we began our time together by sharing stories from our lives, contexts, urban missions, and immersion experiences. These stories show us where God is working to form fresh approaches to urban spirituality and theology. These are stories that give us insight and fill us with hope.

ISUM Working Group participants shared stories where Christian urban leaders and teams exemplify these characteristics (i.e., stories of hope):

Care for urban dwellers and groups, and their wellbeing: Many urban missionaries care for the broken, silenced, ignored, wounded, marginalized, and those at the "bottom of the ladder."

Concern for the real needs of communities: Many urban missionaries meet real needs, are present among people, and build meaningful relationships. They care for whole communities and engage in community development.

Connection with urban communities: Many urban missionaries listen, learn, hear concerns, and communicate authentically. They connect with the needs and insights and histories of the slum communities among whom they serve.

Witness to the kingdom of God in urban settings: Many urban missionaries are people of joy, mercy, hope, justice, love, faith, gentleness, encouragement, and liberation.

Compassion for people and their wellbeing: Many urban missionaries are compassionate servants who are passionate about justice, healing, reconciliation, mercy, mission, and community.

The ISUM Working Group also engaged in three "immersion experiences" in Kuala Lumpur. This involved looking for "signs of hope" in the areas of urban theology and spirituality. We joined in these three immersions experiences:

1. *City Discipleship Presbyterian Church (CDPC).* In obedience to the Great Commission set forth by Jesus, CDPC seeks to help individuals establish good and mature relationships with God and to produce fruitful disciples impacting both their personal life as well as the lives of people around them. Since its establishment in July 2000, CDPC has been collaborating with churches around the Klang Valley to work with the community of Subang Jaya, USJ, and Petaling Jaya. CDPC serves various

communities, ranging from university students to children with learning disabilities.

2. *KingdomCity*. KingdomCity is one church in three cities—Kuala Lumpur in Malaysia, Perth in Western Australia, and Phnom Penh in Cambodia. This church believes everybody deserves to belong. Their heart and vision are to connect, equip, and empower people to bring the reality of God to their world. They're passionate about the miraculous and about transforming communities. They're committed to relevant Christian mission, theology, and spirituality for Kuala Lumpur. KingdomCity sees its own community as a mission-field, filled with people who need Jesus. They believe that God has called them to go beyond their own community to reach people of the world by sharing the love of Christ.

3. *A Theological Seminary in Kuala Lumpur*. I have purposely obscured the name of this seminary. This way, I can describe its ministries while protecting its anonymity. Out of the three immersion experiences, I'll focus on this one here. I'll provide a snapshot of the "signs of hope" present in the way it does urban theology and spirituality.

This theological seminary is committed to equipping pastors, missionaries, and ministry leaders for effective ministry in Asia. The seminary's commitment to holistic training includes equipping leaders to serve among transient urban dwellers in Kuala Lumpur. In this immersion experience, we were able to interview seminary students who have come to Malaysia either as migrant workers or refugees. Ministering in churches of transient urban dwellers poses particular challenges for these young leaders. Training transient urban dwellers for mission and ministry poses other challenges for this theological seminary in Kuala Lumpur.

This innovative Asian theological seminary is exploring fresh approaches to urban mission, theology, spiritual formation, and ministry training. They are training people in new ways to serve and empower transient urban dwellers (e.g., asylum seekers, migrants, refugees, stateless people, people in refugee-like situations, and others of concern).

Kuala Lumpur is a strategic location for this, since it has around 250,000 such people—Myanmarese, Persians, Afghans, Iraqi, Tamils, Indonesians, Somalis, Sri Lankans, Nepalese, and other groups. These arrive in Malaysia and apply for refugee status through the UNHCR (the United Nations refugee agency).

The UNHCR writes the following about Malaysia: "Malaysia has not yet signed the 1951 Refugee Convention or its 1967 Protocol and lacks a formal legislative and administrative framework to address refugee matters. With no work rights, refugees, in particular women and children, tend to be at a high risk of exploitation, particularly refugee children who have no access to government schools. UNHCR works with some partner organizations to support refugee health, education, and community empowerment. However, as the non-governmental sector in Malaysia remains limited, the Office also directly implements activities. The Malaysian Government provides access to public health care at a reduced rate for refugees recognized by UNHCR. The Malaysian Government implements strict policies to deter undocumented migrants from its territory. Since refugees and asylum-seekers aren't distinguished from undocumented migrants under Malaysian law, they are vulnerable to the same penalties, including arrest, detention, and deportation."

This seminary is asking important questions as it trains men and women for mission and ministry. It wants to equip them to build spiritualities and theologies adequate for new urban environments. Here's a sample of some of these questions: What does contextual theology and spirituality look like for particular transient and vulnerable populations? (E.g. Myanmarese, Afghan, Iraqi, Tamil, Indonesian, Somali, Sri Lankan, and Nepalese refugees). How do we do contextual theology, given these groups' sense of attachment and non-attachment to their cultures and societies? (Their feelings about their cultures and societies are often mixed). How do particular missiological themes shape our approaches to theological reflection and spiritual formation? Such themes include holism, transformation, comparative religions, cultural studies, and contextualization. How does Christian theology and spirituality change when individuals and Christian communities immerse themselves in the love, service, and fellowship of the poor and marginalized and transient? What does it mean not only to *read* the Scriptures but also to *do* the Scriptures (individually, as churches, and as theological colleges)?

When this seminary was first planted in Kuala Lumpur, its aim was to train middle class Chinese Christian leaders. Of course, there's nothing wrong with that. But, over time, the focus has shifted to training leaders in urban mission. This is especially training for mission among the urban poor, and among vulnerable people groups. This makes the seminary innovative missiologically. But it's also vulnerable to the fates of these transient, marginalized, and persecuted urban dwellers.

Two students of this seminary illustrate the theological, missional, and spiritual concerns of its faculty and students. Our ISUM Working Group had an opportunity to interview both students. The first is a Myanmarese student and the second is from a country in Western Asia (it's better that I don't name the country).

The Myanmarese student is working with Myanmarese refugee communities in Kuala Lumpur. Many Myanmarese in Malaysia hold a UN card. They are awaiting resettlement in Australia, Europe, or North America. This student holds English language classes and Bible study groups at midnight many nights of the week. (Myanmarese refugees work such long hours that this is the only time they're available for fellowship and training.) People in power "shake down" these refugees regularly (easy money). This makes them fearful, insecure, and uncertain about their incomes and futures. It prevents their children from getting a proper education. This Myanmarese theological student serves among this refugee community. He visits Myanmarese in factories and homes. He provides pastoral support. And he offers theological, biblical, and English language training.

The second student is from a country in Western Asia. Many people from this country arrive legally in Malaysia. They then seek asylum but are prevented from working. Their families struggle to survive. They can't find opportunities for work and education and social connection. There are few churches in Malaysia that cater for people from this country. So, mission activities and worship gatherings among this group are rare. Asylum seekers from this country are often depressed, financially desperate, and lonely. They are often forced to work illegally, and fear arrest and deportation. They are emotionally affected by persecution and violence (both in their home country and since they left). They often don't trust other refugees and asylum seekers from their country. Their country has spies in Malaysia who monitor refugees and asylum seekers. So, they're fearful of the consequences for them and their families in Malaysia and in Western Asia. Another challenge for mission among this group is the reason for their conversion *from* Islam *to* Christianity. Sometimes conversion is *a protest against Islam*, and not a real conversion. The seminary student from this nationality is serving among this group at great personal risk and cost. But he's passionate about mission. And he's committed to healing and reconciliation among people from his country.

All three immersion experiences offered stories of hope and transformation. And we had the opportunity to share stories from our lives, contexts, urban missions, and experiences. Together, these stories show us where God is forming new and life-giving approaches to urban spirituality and theology. These are hope-filled and hopeful stories.

Challenges to Hope

Our 2014 ISUM Working Group focused on *signs of hope in the city*. We focused on stories that give us insight into emerging urban theology and spirituality, and that fill us with hope. But we also consider challenges to such hope. Challenges for robust urban theology and spirituality are widespread. Here are some of them:

Firstly, the presence of dichotomies in the church. (E.g. evangelism vs. social action, conservative vs. emerging forms of theology, and so forth). These dichotomies are often artificial, divisive, and unhelpful.

Secondly, the scarcity of resources and writings on holistic ministry, theology, and spirituality among and for the urban poor.

Thirdly, the dominance of Western forms of theology and spirituality, and the neglect of voices from the Majority World. As C. René Padilla says, "A xeroxed copy of a theology made in Europe or North America can never satisfy the theological needs of the Church in the Third World. Now that the Church has become a world community, the time has come for it to manifest the universality of the Gospel in terms of a theology that isn't bound by a particular culture but shows the many-sided wisdom of God."[50]

Fourthly, superficial attempts at contextualization of theology and spirituality in new urban environments. Again, C. René Padilla writes, "The contextualization of the Gospel can never take place apart from the contextualization of the Church... The truly indigenous Church is the one that through death and resurrection with Christ embodies the Gospel within its own culture. It adopts a way of being, thinking, and acting in which its own cultural patterns are transformed and fulfilled by the Gospel. In a sense, it's the cultural embodiment of Christ formed within a given culture. The task of the Church isn't the extension of a culture of Christianity throughout the world, but the incarnation of the Gospel in each culture... The contextualization of the Gospel won't consist of an adaptation of an existing theology to a given culture. It won't be merely the result of an intellectual process. It won't be aided by a benevolent missionary paternalism intended to help the young church to select those cultural elements that can be regarded as positive. The contextualization of the Gospel can only be a gift of grace granted by God to a church that is seeking to place the totality of life under the lordship of Christ in its historical situation. More than a wonder of nature, the incarnation is a wonder of grace."[51]

Fifthly, the Western nature of so much spiritual and mystical theology. Such theology is often written from a Western, middle-class, suburban, rural, or monastic perspective. Such spiritual theologies—and resources in spiritual formation—are inadequate for urban missionaries. Often, they don't help those serving among the urban poor in densely populated cities.

There are many other challenges to Christian spirituality and theology in a new urban and global world. These aren't insurmountable. But we must take them seriously.

Questions that Emerge for Urban Spirituality and Theology

The world is rapidly urbanizing. More than 6.5 billion people will live in cities by 2050. Most of these urban dwellers will be in developing countries. Around 80 percent of this burgeoning urban population will live in Africa and Asia. The United Nations claims that the world is unprepared for the challenges this will raise for resources—e.g., the increasing demands for energy, water, and sanitation. The world is unprepared for the challenges urban growth raises for public services, land-use, food scarcity, employment, transportation, education, and health.

The church faces its own challenges as the world rapidly urbanizes, and as the church shifts its center of gravity to the Majority World. As Philip Jenkins writes,

"We're currently living through one of the transforming moments in the history of religion worldwide. Over the last five centuries, the story of Christianity has been inextricably bound up with that of Europe and European-derived civilizations overseas, above all in North America. Until recently, the overwhelming majority of Christians have lived in white nations... Over the last century, however, the center of gravity in

---

51 Ibid. 28–30.

the Christian world has shifted inexorably away from Europe, southward, to Africa and Latin America, and eastward, toward Asia. Today, the largest Christian communities on the planet are to be found in those regions."[52]

Urbanization and the shift of the church to the Majority World raise important questions for Christian spirituality and theology. Here are some questions that our ISUM Working Group identified. We didn't seek to answer these questions. But we believe that they are worth further investigation. Our answers to these questions will help us form robust spiritualities and theologies for a new urban world.

Here are the questions we identified:

When we talk about an "urban world", do we mean the poor, marginalized, and exploited, or do we mean all those living in urban settings? And how does this affect our theology and spirituality? Do theology and spirituality look different for different groups living in urban settings?

What's the point of Christian theologies and spiritualities specific to an urban world? And how do we pursue and practice Christian theologies and spiritualities specific to urban environments?

How do Christians put Christian spirituality and other spiritualities into conversation?

How do Christians lead with the Spirit cross-culturally?

What should be the role of a privileged Western person in a developing community? How can such a person join in the shaping of indigenous Christian spiritualities and theologies?

How can theology be multi-voiced and multi-peopled?

How can we know Jesus more deeply when serving with the urban poor? How can we express this relationship through our spirituality and theology?

---

[52] Jenkins, *The Next Christendom*, 1.

How are theology and spirituality enhanced through food, laughter, tears, celebration, rituals, and community development in a new urban world?

What does spiritual formation look like in an urban world and among the urban poor? Much of the literature on spiritual formation suggests a quiet and tranquil setting. But the settings urban missionaries serve in are densely populated. And people have little free time and personal space. What do rest, peace, and spirituality look like in noisy, busy, mega-cities and slum settings?

How do theology and spirituality change in the context of urban mission and service? How do they grow, mature, and deepen?

How do we find rest and stillness in the city (stillness in the midst of cacophony and frenetic activity)?

How does the urban church connect urban theology, urban mission, and urban spirituality?

What does it mean for the urban church to move from invitation (evangelism and social concern) *to* hospitality (discipleship and welcome) *to* embrace (reconciliation and community)?

What processes facilitate the growth of theology and spirituality relevant to particular urban communities?

What is the meaning of the incarnation, the cross, and the resurrection in the context of urban poverty?

What do theology and spirituality look like when they are relevant to specific communities and contexts?

What does spiritual warfare look like in urban settings, slum communities, and among the poor and marginalized?

How do we create a spirituality that sustains and inspires not just "expats"—that is, not just a small, foreign, Christian group living among the poor—but everyone in that context?

How do spirituality and theology connect with the *reason* we do what we do among the urban poor?

What does it mean to be a part of a kingdom of peace and non-violence? And to be witnesses of the now-but-not-yet of the kingdom of God? How does this shape Christian theology and spirituality?

What does it mean to formulate theology and spirituality *in* urban practices?

What aspects of spirituality and theology does our mission within urban settings illuminate?

How can we embody faithful theological practices that deepen our spirituality? And what can we do to make this possible in our communities?

As we live and serve among the urban poor, how can we live between grief and hope, between exhaustion and renewal, between isolation and community, between the present realities and the coming kingdom?

How do we *live out* and *live in* the kingdom of God in a new urban world?

These are just some of the questions that a new urban world raises for Christian spirituality and theology. The church will enrich its theology and spiritual vitality as it explores these questions through local-global conversations.

A Call to Action: Nurturing Spirituality and Theology in an Urban Context

At the end of our few days together, our ISUM Working Group discussed how we might form new practices and habits that enhance urban Christian spirituality and theology. We offer these here as a "call to action". They are recommendations to the broader church. The Christian church—and especially the urban church—needs to do the following over the next decade:

- Explore fresh ways to nurture urban Christian spiritualities and theologies. We need ones that sustain, challenge, and inspire those living and working among the urban poor. These urban missionaries need spiritual and theological resources. They need help to express the kingdom of God in their communities and draw people into the ways of the kingdom.

- Discover ways in which a lifestyle of peace enhances spirituality, theology, and mission in a new urban world. A peace-filled Christian lifestyle is less frenetic and "blindly active".

- Gather examples of ways those working and living among the urban poor express Christian spiritual practices and disciplines. Learn from these examples. Develop resources and tools that sustain urban mission, urban communities, and urban faith.

- Expand our ideas and practices of prayer in urban contexts. Appreciate how prayer is practiced among and with the poorest of the poor, in some of the largest and most densely populated cities of the world.

- Investigate practical and rigorous answers to the questions our ISUM Working Group proposed above. (See "Questions that Emerge for Urban Spirituality and Theology".) Don't just come up with theoretical answers. Pursue local and concrete practices and responses.

- Address the "challenges to hope" identified by our ISUM Working Group. (See the section above on "Challenges to Hope".)

- Support the church to fulfil her urban mission and the missional mandate God has given her in the world. Seek to be a Bride without blemish. Such a church puts faith and love into action. It witnesses to the kingdom of God on earth. And it does this through liberating forms of urban mission, theology, and faith.

- Facilitate Christian spirituality that emerges within built environments—cultures, poverty, buildings, smells, noise, connections, etc. Discern where God is at work there.

- Discover how poverty, difficulties, and challenges provide opportunities for connections, mission, and justice. Trials and troubles often bring people together—the Spirit is present and working.

- Find ways to be agents of peace, justice, hope, and reconciliation in urban settings. Witness to the kingdom of God amidst the brokenness, injustices, and woundedness of cities.

- Understand that love is better than mere theories, theologies, or strategies. Genuine love is better than "best practices". Let this truth permeate the urban church's spirituality, mission, and theology.

- Foster a lifestyle of invitation, hospitality, and embrace (even of enemies and persecutors).

- Cultivate habits of quietness and stillness (internal and external). Do this through personal and communal spirituality. And do this in the midst of the noise, busyness, and chaotic natures of large urban centers.

- Nurture capacities for celebration, lament, liberation, and meaning-making in urban settings. Such practices can enrich both churches and their local communities.

- Explore ways to make Jesus infectious in diverse, pluralistic, and sometimes hostile environments.

- Develop a deeper theology of the kingdom and an associated kingdom-oriented Christian spirituality. Ask, "What does it mean to be a part of a kingdom of peace, hope, reconciliation, justice, love, and non-violence?" And "How can the urban church witness to the now-but-not-yet of the kingdom of God?"

- Celebrate being in diverse and urban contexts. Form Christian spiritualities and theologies characterized by peace-making, truth-telling, and justice-bringing, but also by celebration. Celebrate a wide range of things, such as those that follow. (1) In slum areas there's hardship, poverty, and suffering. But there's also community, love, and joy. (2) We can celebrate the food, languages, relationships, innovations, and cultures in urban settings. (3) The urban context is often invigorating. It brings energy. And it can make us aware of God, life, humanity, redemption, and personal and communal transformation. (4) We can celebrate how urban and diverse contexts enlarge our faith, spirituality, and theology. If we let them, they can inspire the church to be truly ecumenical, multi-racial, multi-cultural, multi-peopled, and multi-voiced. There are so many things we can celebrate about being in new urban settings. (And we celebrate while striving to be agents of peace, healing, and change where there is sin and brokenness.)

- Develop a theology and spirituality of missional engagement. This sustains urban faith, discipleship, obedience, community, and mission amidst suffering, struggle, liberation, and celebration.

Orlando E. Costas writes, "To take head on oppressive structures like consumerism, technology, militarism, multinational capitalism, international communism, racism, and sexism, we need a *spirituality of missional engagement*: a devotional attitude, a personal ethic, a continuous liturgical experience that flows out of and expresses itself in apostolic obedience. Prayer, Bible study, personal ethics, and worship won't mean withdrawal from the world but *immersion in its suffering and struggles.* Likewise, participation in the struggles of history won't mean an abandonment of piety and contemplation, but an experience of God from the depths of human suffering.

Mission without spirituality can't survive any more than combustion without oxygen. The nature of the world in which we live and the gospel that we have been committed to communicate therein demand, however, *that it be a spirituality of engagement not of withdrawal.* Such a spirituality can only be cultivated in obedience and discipleship, and not in the isolated comfort of one's inner self. By the same token, it can only be verified in the liberating struggles against the principalities and powers that hold so many millions in bondage."[53]

---

[53] Costas, *Christ Outside the Gate*, 171–72. Italics added for emphasis.

7. Missions on the Move: Ten Global Shifts in Christian Mission

Recently, I did a radio interview on ten global shifts in Christian mission. Here's the transcript.

Introduction

Host: Hello and welcome! Today, we're exploring the changes worldwide in Christian mission: the new directions and trends shaping how the church engages in outreach globally. Our guest is a lifelong missionary and researcher who has witnessed these changes firsthand. We'll be discussing ten key shifts in global Christian mission, each paired with a real story that brings it to life. Thank you for joining us.

Graham: Thank you for having me. I'm excited to talk about these remarkable changes in global mission and share some inspiring stories. Recently, I published a book called *World Christianity: An Introduction.*[54] The landscape of Christian mission is evolving in amazing ways, from digital mission to microchurches. These changes are truly global, affecting every continent and denomination, and they demonstrate how the Good News is being shared in our rapidly changing world.

The ten global shifts in Christian mission are:

1. Embracing Digital Missions
2. Mission in the Migration Era
3. The Rise of Reverse Mission
4. Local Leadership and Indigenous Mission

---

[54] Hill, *World Christianity.*

5. Creation Care as Mission

6. Mission Becomes Polycentric

7. Integral Mission: Word, Sign, and Deed Together

8. Spirit-Empowered Mission

9. Church Planting Movements and Rapid Multiplication

10. Microchurches and Fresh Expressions

Embracing Digital Missions

Host: The first significant change is something many of us experience daily: digital technology. How has digital evangelism and mission changed the way Christians engage in mission, and do you have a story that illustrates its impact?

Graham: Absolutely. Digital evangelism and mission (sharing the gospel through the internet, social media, and other technologies) has opened a vast new mission field. With billions of people online, the church can reach individuals far beyond physical walls.[55] One powerful story comes from a recent online prayer campaign. A young man, feeling utterly alone and suicidal, went on social media to post what he thought would be a final goodbye. At that critical moment, he saw an ad from a Christian group offering to pray for anyone in need. It simply said, "We care about you. Can we pray for you?"[56] That caught his attention. He responded, shared his struggles, and a church online prayer team began praying with him. In that moment of virtual connection, he realized he wasn't invisible: people cared, and God cared. As they prayed, he felt hope spark for the first time in ages and found the courage to step back from the brink.[57] Today, he's alive and doing much better, connected to an online faith community. This story illustrates the transformative power of digital mission: when prayer meets technology, it can reach people right where they are, even in their darkest hour.[58]

---

[55] Kim, "Embracing Digital Evangelism."
[56] Kim, "Embracing Digital Evangelism."
[57] Kim, "Embracing Digital Evangelism."
[58] Kim, "Embracing Digital Evangelism."

Digital evangelism takes many forms: from evangelistic YouTube videos and Bible apps, to virtual church services and WhatsApp prayer groups. It enables Christians to engage with seekers in a personal and anonymous manner. For example, someone curious about Jesus in a country with few churches might find a Christian podcast or Instagram post and start asking questions. We're seeing churches train "digital missionaries" to engage in online forums and comment sections. The beauty is that the gospel is just one click away. A recent study noted that online searches for spiritual topics increased during the pandemic, suggesting a significant opportunity.[59] In short, digital tools are redefining missions outreach: breaking down geographic and social barriers so that the good news of Christ can reach people on their phones and screens worldwide. The story of that young man reminds us that God can use a Facebook ad or a chat message to save a life. This is a new frontier for mission, and it's happening now on a global scale.

Mission in the Migration Era

Host: The following change is driven by global migration. People are moving all over the world. How is migration-driven mission shaping the church, and can you share a story about that?

Graham: We're in an age of unprecedented human mobility: refugees fleeing wars, students studying abroad, workers seeking jobs overseas. This diaspora of peoples is having a considerable impact on mission. God is essentially bringing the mission field to our neighborhoods. One clear example is the Syrian refugee crisis. During the height of that crisis, thousands of displaced Syrian Muslims encountered the love of Christ through Christian relief agencies and local churches.[60] Let me share a composite story based on many true accounts: imagine a Syrian family who fled their war-torn home and ended up in a camp in Greece. They arrive traumatized, having lost everything. In that

59 Kim, "Embracing Digital Evangelism."
60 YWAM Salem. "How Refugees Transform Christianity."

camp, a group of Christian aid workers (many of whom are local Greek church volunteers) welcome the family with food, blankets, and medical assistance. But they offer more than physical aid; they show genuine friendship, listening to the family's sorrows and praying for them in Jesus's name. Over time, the refugee family is amazed: these Christians care for us even though we're strangers and come from a different faith. That kind of unexpected love has opened many hearts. I've heard of a Syrian mother who asked, "Why do you do this for us?" and the volunteer replied, "Because Jesus loves you." Moments like that have led some refugees to begin reading the Bible and even to come to faith in Christ. In fact, relief organizations noted that a significant portion of frontline caregivers were Christians, which "opened doors for the gospel in ways traditional evangelism never could."[61]

Migration-driven mission isn't just about refugees finding Christ; it's also about Christians on the move. Consider a Christian nurse from the Philippines who migrates to Saudi Arabia for work. She might quietly share Christ's love with coworkers or start a small Bible study with other migrants. Or an Indian IT professional in Dubai who leads an underground house church for fellow expatriates. These diaspora believers often become "accidental missionaries", bringing their faith into lands where traditional missionaries can't easily go.

Meanwhile, in Western countries, immigrants from Asia, Africa, and Latin America are revitalizing churches. Immigrant congregations are growing in cities such as London, Toronto, and Sydney, and they often reach out to other ethnic communities and native communities alike. So, migration has made mission multi-directional: it's no longer from one "Christian" country to another land. It's happening everywhere: Middle Eastern refugees in Europe meeting Jesus, Latin American believers planting churches in the Middle East, and so on. The Great Commission is being carried out in trains and planes, refugee camps and college dorms. Wherever people move, God is at work. The

---

[61] YWAM Salem. "How Refugees Transform Christianity."

story of that Syrian family is just one of many showing how the movement of people can lead to the movement of the gospel, transforming both those who go and the communities that receive them.

The Rise of Reverse Mission

Host: That leads us to "reverse mission." We often think of missionaries as going from the West to other parts of the world, but reverse mission flips that. What is reverse mission, and do you have a story of how it's unfolding?

Graham: Reverse mission is an exciting phenomenon: it's when Christians from regions that have historically received missionaries (such as Africa, Asia, and Latin America) are now missionaries to the West. It reflects a significant shift in Christianity's center of gravity. Today, over two-thirds of all Christians reside in the Global South, rather than in North America or Europe.[62] With that growth, believers from these regions feel called to share the gospel abroad, including in countries where Christianity was first introduced to them. One striking story is of a Nigerian pastor (I'll call him Daniel) who moved to England. Daniel's wife had a vivid dream of him preaching to a large crowd of English people in a snowy town: a place unlike their native Lagos, which never sees snow. They took it as a sign that God was sending them to the UK. Sure enough, Daniel ended up in a city in northern England. He started a church in a community center, and initially, it was mostly fellow African immigrants who attended. But Daniel was determined to reach his English neighbors. He went out of his way to be a good neighbor: helping people carry groceries, learning to enjoy tea time, and even sending Christmas cards. Slowly, locals grew to trust him. Today, his church, aptly named Hope Centre, includes not just Africans but also white British folks who had little prior church experience. This is a real-

---

[62] Cheng-Tozun, "What Majority-World Missions Really Looks Like."

life example of a reverse mission: a pastor from Africa rekindling faith in a post-Christian Western context.[63]

And it's not an isolated case. In fact, in the early 2000s, the largest church in Kyiv, Ukraine, was led by a Nigerian missionary, and the largest church in England was pastored by an African as well.[64] African and Latin American churches are actively sending missionaries to Europe, North America, and other regions that were once strongholds of Christianity but are now more secular. For instance, there are over 240 African majority churches in London's Southwark borough alone (some operating in former pubs or cinemas), and they're not just serving African expatriates but also evangelizing British locals.[65] I'm aware of a Brazilian missionary family planting a church in Portugal, as well as Korean evangelists conducting outreach in California. These "reverse missionaries" often claim they are "bringing the fire back" to lands where church attendance has declined.[66] It's quite humbling and beautiful: the gospel has come full circle. Countries that once sent missionaries now receive them in return. Reverse mission shows that in the body of Christ, there's no part of the world so spiritually rich that others can't bless it. Every nation can be both a sender and a receiver. As one Ethiopian pastor in London said, "Britain brought us the gospel; now God has brought us here when Christianity is challenged [in Britain]. It's not a coincidence we're here."[67] That sense of destiny fuels reverse missionaries. So, this trend is revitalizing Western churches and reminding all of us that the Great Commission is from everywhere to everywhere: truly a global, shared mission.

---

63 Kuo, "Africa's 'Reverse Missionaries'."
64 Akaeze, "Fire from Africa."
65 Kuo, "Africa's 'Reverse Missionaries'."
66 Kuo, "Africa's 'Reverse Missionaries'."
67 Kuo, "Africa's 'Reverse Missionaries'."

Local Leadership and Indigenous Mission

Host: Another key change is a shift toward local leadership in missions. What does that look like, and can you share a story about empowering indigenous leaders?

Graham: This is a vital development. In the past, mission work often meant foreign missionaries leading the churches or organizations they started abroad. Today, there's a much greater emphasis on raising up local Christian leaders to lead their own people. The goal is for churches to be self-governing, self-supporting, and self-propagating: an idea that missiologists refer to as the "three-self" principle for indigenous churches.[68] Practically, this means a missionary's job is increasingly to train and mentor, then step aside as soon as local believers are ready to take charge. Let me illustrate with a story. In a rural village in Cambodia, a mission agency started a small school and church years ago.

Initially, Western missionaries pastored the church. But they intentionally discipled a young woman from that village (let's call her Sopheak) who was passionate about her people. Sopheak received biblical training and gradually assumed more responsibility, progressing from teaching children's classes to leading prayer meetings. Within a few years, the church that once depended on foreign leadership had Sopheak as its pastor. She preaches in the local language, understands the culture intuitively, and has a heart to serve her neighbors. Under her leadership, the church has grown and even started sending its own members to share the gospel in nearby villages. The foreign missionaries gladly moved into supportive roles and eventually on to new areas, knowing the church is in capable local hands. This kind of handover to indigenous leadership is happening across the world in Christian missions.[69]

One remarkable outcome is that local-led ministries often thrive and multiply in ways outsiders never could. Local leaders bring cultural insight and credibility to the table. They can navigate linguistic nuances

---

68 Wikipedia, "Indigenous Church Mission Theory."
69 Wikipedia, "Indigenous Church Mission Theory."

and community relationships naturally. For example, in India, many church-planting movements are led entirely by Indian believers. Some movements have seen tens of thousands of new house churches because they empower every local disciple to lead others. In fact, there have been reports of movements in North India, where over 40,000 churches were established in 15 years under local leadership, following the shift of missionaries to coaching roles.[70] Globally, the majority of missionaries are now from non-Western countries, and they often partner with Westerners in equal roles rather than subservient ones.[71] I've visited an African-led mission organization in Kenya that hosts missionaries from America, flipping the old script! The key idea is partnership: the body of Christ working together, but letting those closest to the context lead. This change also respects the dignity and gifts God has given every culture. As Western missionaries, we've learned humility: that our way isn't the only way. By focusing on local leadership, missions become more sustainable. The churches aren't seen as foreign implants but truly belong to their community. And as Sopheak's story shows, an indigenous church can stand on its own and even send out its own missionaries. Ultimately, empowering local leaders makes the church more rooted, resilient, and reproducible everywhere.

Creation Care as Mission

Host: The fifth change is an interesting one: creation care. People often fail to connect environmental stewardship with Christian mission. How is caring for creation becoming part of mission work, and can you give an example?

Graham: You're right: traditionally, mission was often thought of only in terms of saving souls, sometimes without much regard for environmental or social issues. However, a growing movement of Christians worldwide views creation care (caring for the environment) as

---

[70] Kiser, "David Watson and Church Planting Movements."
[71] Cheng-Tozun, "What Majority-World Missions Really Looks Like."

an integral part of their mission and witness. The logic is straightforward: if we believe God created the world and declared it good, then taking care of the earth and addressing problems such as pollution and climate change is part of loving our neighbors and honoring the Creator. This is sometimes referred to as "integral creation care" within the mission. A vivid story comes from Ghana, West Africa. There's a forest there called the Atewa Forest, rich in biodiversity and a source of water for millions. A few years ago, that forest was under threat: slated for mining for minerals. A Christian conservation organization called A Rocha Ghana decided to act. They saw that defending this forest was defending God's creation and protecting local communities' livelihood. It was a real David-and-Goliath battle: on one side, the government and a big foreign company eyeing short-term profit; on the other side, a small band of Christians armed with faith, science, and a passion for justice. A Rocha Ghana mobilized villagers, conducted scientific research, and launched a campaign to save the forest. They lobbied politicians, raised public awareness, and even pursued legal action. Amazingly, their effort succeeded in halting the mining project (at least so far), protecting the forest from destruction.[72] The director of that group, Seth, said, "This is a practical demonstration of our faith in the God of creation and our role as stewards of God's earth."[73] That's a powerful statement: caring for a forest became a witness of Christian faith in action.

This integration of creation care in mission is happening in many places. In Mongolia, missionaries and local Christians are responding to deadly air pollution by distributing efficient stoves and planting trees, demonstrating Christ's love tangibly.[74] In the Philippines, churches lead coastal clean-ups and mangrove planting efforts, which not only restore fisheries for hungry communities but also open hearts to the gospel message of hope and restoration. I've seen young Christians, especially those in Gen Z and Millennials, resonate with this. Climate change is a

---

[72] Bookless, et al., "Creation Care."
[73] Bookless, et al., "Creation Care."
[74] Bookless, et al., "Creation Care."

global concern, and when the church steps up to address it, it speaks volumes. In fact, nearly two-thirds of evangelical leaders say they've preached on our responsibility to care for God's creation.[75] It's becoming mainstream. Creation care is framed as both loving the "least of these" (since environmental damage disproportionately affects the poor) and as a witness: when Christians plant gardens, conserve water, or defend an ecosystem, people notice that our faith isn't just otherworldly; it cares about all of life. One could argue that creation care serves as a new apologetic for mission: when we take the earth seriously, many will take the gospel seriously.[76] Whether it's installing solar panels on church roofs, teaching sustainable farming to rural families, or advocating for clean water, caring for creation has become a vital part of Christian mission. It's holistic: we proclaim and demonstrate the good news that Jesus is Lord of all creation, and he brings restoration not just to souls but to the whole world.

Mission Becomes Polycentric

Host: Let's talk about a polycentric mission. That's a fancy term: what does it mean, and how is mission becoming polycentric around the world?

Graham: A polycentric mission means there is no single "hub" or center of missionary activity; instead, there are multiple centers of sending and receiving. In other words, the age when Europe or America was the clear center of global mission is over. The Christian mission movement has numerous centers, including locations such as Seoul, São Paulo, Lagos, and Manila, all of which serve as major launching points for missions today. Mission is "from everywhere to everywhere." We touched on this with reverse mission and migration, but polycentric mission is broader. It's about collaboration across the global church as equal partners. A notable example is an international missions

---

[75] Randall, "Preaching That Connects Creation Care to Climate Change."
[76] Bookless, et al., "Creation Care."

conference I recently attended. The planning committee comprised leaders from five continents: a Brazilian evangelist, a Nigerian theologian, a Korean pastor, an American missiologist, and an Indian church planter. They were designing a strategy together. That wouldn't have happened a few generations ago. Today, it's normal. At the conference, I met young missionaries from Latin America who were preparing to serve in the Middle East, as well as Africans and Asians coordinating mission work in Europe. This truly reflects that Christianity's center of energy has shifted. Consider this statistic: in 2015, nine of the top 20 countries sending out Christian missionaries were in the Majority World (Global South), including nations such as Brazil, India, South Korea, Nigeria, and the Philippines, all of which ranked in the top 20.[77] And while the United States still sends the most significant number, Western missionary numbers are declining, whereas non-Western missionary numbers are rapidly increasing.[78]

Polycentric mission also appears in how mission agencies operate. Many Western mission organizations now have leadership or board members from Asia or Africa. Some have even moved their headquarters or training centers overseas to be nearer to where the church is growing fastest. For example, the Lausanne Movement, which connects evangelicals globally, deliberately holds its gatherings on different continents (such as Cape Town in 2010 or Asia for the next one) to ensure a diverse range of perspectives. And mission networks are emerging that are led by the Global South, such as the Movement for African National Initiatives (MANI) or the Latin American Missions Network, which coordinate efforts across countries. What this means practically is better mutual learning. A church in Egypt may learn from a church in Brazil how to conduct youth ministry, while a church in Canada may learn from a church in Kenya about community

---

[77] Cheng-Tozun, "What Majority-World Missions Really Looks Like."
[78] Cheng-Tozun, "What Majority-World Missions Really Looks Like."

development. The flow of ideas and personnel is no longer one-way; it's multidirectional.

Let me share a small story to illustrate the spirit of polycentric mission. A few years ago, an American church partnered with a Kenyan church to reach street kids in Nairobi. Initially, the Americans assumed they'd provide funds and models, and the Kenyans would implement. However, the Kenyans had their own successful methods and ultimately trained the Americans in relational outreach and prayer practices that proved remarkably effective. Now that the partnership has morphed, they occasionally send Kenyan short-term mission teams to serve in American inner cities, applying some of those lessons in a Western context! I found that beautiful and surprising. It demonstrates how each part of the global church has unique gifts to share, and when we listen to one another, the mission becomes richer. Polycentric mission is essentially the fulfillment of the idea that every nation will play its part in God's mission. It's the whole church taking the whole gospel to the entire world, together. No single country or culture is in charge: Christ is the head, and we all follow. This change is making the mission more collaborative, culturally attuned, and globally owned than ever before.

Integral Mission: Word, Sign, and Deed Together

Host: The seventh trend you identified is integral mission (also called holistic mission). What is integral mission, and do you have a story of how combining word and deed is impacting communities?

Graham: Integral mission is the idea that Christian mission should address the whole person (both spiritual and physical needs) rather than treating evangelism and social action as separate tasks. It's summed up as "Whole Gospel for the whole person through the whole church." In the 1970s, evangelical leaders such as John Stott and René Padilla championed this approach, and it's now widely embraced across denominations. Practically, integral mission means preaching the love of Christ and demonstrating it through compassion and justice. It's feeding the hungry and also offering the "bread of life." It involves praying with the sick and providing medicine. The story I want to share comes from a rural community in Nigeria. There, a local pastor (Venerable Isaac was his name) had a small church that realized preaching on Sundays alone wasn't transforming their impoverished village. So they asked a bold question: "If we were to do ministry exactly as Jesus did, what would it look like?"[79] Jesus, after all, healed and taught, fed and preached. This question led them to change their whole approach. The church became very participatory with the community, mobilizing local resources and talents. They started a health clinic because medical care was hours away; church members volunteered, and some trained as health workers. They also opened a primary school because many children weren't receiving an education. Over the years, this holistic approach yielded incredible results: teenage marriages and pregnancies declined, fewer families were broken, and relationships between men and women in the village improved.[80] Why? Because as they met practical needs, they also taught biblical principles of dignity, mutual respect, and God's plan for families. The whole community was uplifted. And importantly, people's hearts opened to Christ. Many who benefited from the clinic and school began attending church, and they encountered the gospel in word and deed.

The transformation of this Nigerian community was so striking that other church leaders and even secular organizations came to learn from them.[81] That is integral mission in action. It's not just a human development project: it's holistic redemption. I've seen similar stories elsewhere: for example, in a Central American city plagued by gang violence, churches started job training programs for at-risk youth alongside their evangelism. The result was that young people found employment and purpose, left gang life, and also came to faith. Crime rates dropped, and those neighborhoods have active churches now filled with former gang members whose lives have changed. Integral mission is based on Jesus's model: he preached the kingdom and healed the sick

---

79 Tearfund USA. "How Integral Mission Creates Lasting Change."
80 Tearfund USA. "How Integral Mission Creates Lasting Change."
81 Tearfund USA. "How Integral Mission Creates Lasting Change."

and fed the hungry. The early church did the same, caring for widows and orphans while spreading the gospel. We're rediscovering that integration today. Organizations like Tearfund and World Vision explicitly build both evangelism and social action into their mission. They've found that demonstrating God's love through action validates the proclamation of God's love. As the Book of James says, faith without works is dead – and in mission, preaching without love in action often falls flat. However, when a community witnesses the church digging wells for clean water and also sharing the message of the Living Water (Christ), it powerfully reflects the gospel.

One more quick example: A missionary doctor set up a clinic in a poor village in Southeast Asia. He treated illnesses, but he also prayed with each patient. Over time, that clinic became the nucleus of a new church: people encountered Jesus's healing for body and soul there. This approach has meant that churches are building schools, hospitals, and caring for creation, while also advocating for justice: all as part of their mission. It's a beautiful, biblically balanced approach. Integral mission essentially states that there's no bifurcation: saving souls and serving society go hand in hand. And the result is lasting change: not only are individuals saved, but communities are transformed, and God's name is glorified in every sphere of life.

Spirit-Empowered Mission

Host: Many of our listeners come from Pentecostal or charismatic backgrounds, so they'll be familiar with the following change: the surge of Spirit-empowered mission. How is the Holy Spirit moving in missions, and do you have a story that highlights miracles or Spirit-led growth?

Graham: Yes, this is a vast and exciting part of global mission today. The Pentecostal and charismatic movement, which emphasizes the power and gifts of the Holy Spirit, has been experiencing rapid growth worldwide. In fact, Pentecostalism has been one of the fastest-growing segments of Christianity in the Global South. With that growth comes a fresh focus on the Holy Spirit's role in mission. Spirit-empowered mission means relying on the Spirit for guidance, boldness, and even supernatural confirmations of the message (like healing, prophecy, deliverance). Essentially, it's a mission with the Book of Acts as a present reality, not just a historical chapter. I've heard countless modern-day "Acts" stories.

Let me share one that still gives me chills: In a poor region of North India, a group of Christian women runs a small sewing business as a ministry (they employ women of different faiths and treat them with Christ's love). One day, a massive fire broke out in a slum neighborhood where many of their employees lived. The flames spread rapidly, threatening to consume hundreds of little homes. Some of the Christian women were there and immediately started helping neighbors throw water and rescue belongings. Others, who were off-site, gathered and prayed fervently (by name) for each of their coworkers' households as the fire raged.[82] They asked Jesus to protect those specific homes. By nightfall, the fire was finally doused. The next morning, as they all came together, they discovered something astonishing. Every single house belonging to one of their employees was spared, still standing amidst the charred ruins of the neighborhood![83] They could hardly believe it. Their Hindu and Muslim colleagues had joined in those prayers too, and now saw that the name of Jesus had power. This miracle opened the door for many conversations about faith, and some of those families began attending a local house church. This true story illustrates how yielding to the Spirit can lead to miracles that authenticate the gospel message.[84]

Such stories are familiar wherever the church expects the Holy Spirit to move. In parts of Africa, it's not unusual to hear of a village coming to Christ because one man was raised from a deathbed or a woman known to be blind suddenly received sight through prayer in Jesus's name. In the Muslim world, there are numerous testimonies of people having dreams and visions of Jesus leading them to seek out

---

82 Hoppe, "6 Stories of God's Holy Spirit."
83 Hoppe, "6 Stories of God's Holy Spirit."
84 Hoppe, "6 Stories of God's Holy Spirit."

Christians and eventually convert: things that human missionaries could never orchestrate, but the Spirit does. A well-known mission researcher noted that in many church-planting movements, miraculous healings or deliverances were a significant factor in initial conversions; the supernatural acts as a bell that draws the curious to hear the gospel.

Spirit-empowered mission also means deep prayer. Many of these fast-growing mission movements are rooted in extraordinary prayer and fasting. For example, church planters in parts of China or Nigeria often spend hours daily in prayer, listening for the Spirit's direction on where to go or who to speak to. There are accounts of missionaries feeling prompted by the Spirit to take a certain road or talk to a particular person, which leads them to someone whom God had prepared. One friend of mine in the Middle East regularly prays for guidance each morning and has experienced "holy Spirit appointments": like meeting a stranger who the night before prayed, "God, if you're real, send someone to me." The Spirit truly is the ultimate director of missions. And of course, Pentecostal worship and zeal bring an energy that fuels evangelism. Places that had been resistant to more formal missionary approaches have been swept up by lively, Spirit-filled house churches where there is joyful music, praying for the sick, and an expectation that God is present and powerful.

Let's not forget that the fastest-growing churches in the world today are often found among Spirit-filled communities. Take Nepal, which has one of the fastest-growing Christian populations: many of those new believers are part of Pentecostal-style churches where healing and prophecy are common. Latin America has seen whole regions turn to Christ amidst signs and wonders. And all of this resonates strongly with Pentecostal and evangelical listeners who know that mission isn't by our strength or cleverness alone, but "by my Spirit, says the Lord." The story of those houses spared from fire demonstrates the same truth Elijah experienced on Mount Carmel: the living God answers by fire (or, in this case, protects from fire), and people then proclaim, "The Lord is God." So, Spirit-empowered mission is essentially a return to the New

Testament expectation that God backs up the preaching of the word with power. It's a trend that's here to stay, and it's drawing multitudes into the kingdom in our time.

Church Planting Movements and Rapid Multiplication

Host: A more traditional-sounding strategy, but one that's being done in new ways, is church planting. Is church planting still a key focus in global mission, and how are we seeing it happen differently now?

Graham: Yes, church planting (starting new worshiping communities) remains at the heart of mission, but the scale and method have evolved. In recent decades, we've seen the rise of what are called Church Planting Movements (CPMs) or Disciple Making Movements (DMMs). These are extraordinary, rapidly multiplying networks of house churches, often in places where Christianity was previously small or nonexistent. Instead of planting one church at a time with a whole building and paid pastor, these movements emphasize simple, reproducible models: small groups meeting in homes, under trees, in coffee shops (anywhere) led by ordinary believers. When one group grows, they mentor new leaders and multiply into two or three groups, and so on. The growth can be exponential. Let me provide a real-life example: In North India, a pioneering missionary named David Watson implemented this approach several years ago. Over the course of approximately 15 years, the movement he helped catalyze reportedly led to the establishment of 40,000 new churches.[85] Yes, 40,000: it sounds almost unbelievable, but when each church is a small community and each one starts others, the numbers add up fast. Those churches collectively resulted in around 12 million new disciples of Christ during that timeframe.[86] And this was in an area that had previously been very unreached. How did it happen? By empowering every convert to immediately become a disciple-maker for their family and friends,

---

[85] Kiser, "David Watson and Church Planting Movements."
[86] Kiser, "David Watson and Church Planting Movements."

keeping structures simple (no need for significant buildings or seminary-trained pastors), and focusing on obedience to Jesus's commands.

Another striking case is Nepal. In 1950, Nepal was a Hindu kingdom with virtually no Christians: perhaps a handful at most. By 2020, some researchers estimate that there are over a million Christians there. In fact, the Christian population in Nepal has risen nearly 40% in the last decade alone, making it one of the fastest-growing Christian communities in the world.[87] This growth has been driven by fervent evangelism and a constant commitment to church planting. Nepali believers, many of whom are first-generation Christians, take the gospel to remote villages, often on foot through the mountains, praying for the sick and sharing the message of Christ. They start little house churches that multiply. I visited Nepal and met a farmer who had started churches in about 20 villages over the course of a few years: he wasn't a traditionally trained pastor, just a man on fire for Jesus who couldn't keep the good news to himself. That passion is typical in church planting movements.

One more story: In China during the 1980s and 1990s, despite persecution, the underground house church movement experienced explosive growth. Small cell churches continued to multiply, often under the radar. One famous network in central China was reported to have grown from a few hundred believers to over a million in about 20 years, purely through believers leading relatives and neighbors to Christ and forming home gatherings. Prayer and the Holy Spirit's work were crucial (tying back to the last point), but also a deliberate strategy of planting churches that plant churches. These movements often exhibit what we call "4th generation" growth and beyond: meaning a church starts a church (2nd generation), which starts another (3rd generation), and another (4th generation), and so on, like a spiritual family tree branching out. Once you hit multiple generations, you know a movement has its own momentum.

---

[87] Hearth, "Christian Population Rises."

What's new in church planting today is also greater collaboration and planning. There are global networks, such as Exponential or New Frontiers, that share best practices for planting churches, whether traditional or micro. Even established denominations are getting on board: many Baptist, Methodist, or Pentecostal denominations have fresh goals to plant hundreds of new congregations in the coming years, often by empowering lay leaders and using unconventional venues. We also see a growing focus on urban church planting, driven by global urbanization, which involves starting churches in apartment complexes, on campuses, and even in businesses. And there's emphasis on unreached people groups: targeting ethnic groups or regions with no church presence by planting the first church there.

Church planting remains centered on the Great Commission: making disciples of all nations. However, the methods have evolved: it might resemble a simple Bible study in a factory dormitory that eventually becomes a church, or a network of family prayer groups in a Muslim-majority area that quietly identify as churches. It's not always the steeple and Sunday service model. The common thread in these new expressions is the aim to be reproducible and indigenous. The fact that one new believer in a movement was noted to have planted 42 churches in one year is astonishing: it tells us that, with the Holy Spirit and a bold vision, the potential for multiplication is enormous.[88] So, yes, church planting is alive and well, but it's less about missionaries building one congregation over five years and more about catalyzing disciples to multiply communities everywhere. It's exciting: it feels like the Book of Acts continued.

Microchurches and Fresh Expressions

Host: Finally, let's talk about microchurches and "fresh expressions" of church. What are these, and how are they changing the face of Christian mission?

---

[88] Garrison, *Church Planting Movements.*

Graham: Microchurches and fresh expressions refer to new, creative forms of Christian community that are typically small, flexible, and aimed at people who might never walk into a traditional church. They're essentially a church in the wild: outside the conventional church building and Sunday service format. This trend is huge in the West (for reaching secular or unchurched people), but also globally as Christians innovate. A microchurch might be a gathering of 5-20 people in a home or a neutral venue, such as a café, gym, park, or even online. A "fresh expression" is a term that came out of the UK (the Church of England and others) to describe new forms of church for a changing culture. Both emphasize meeting people where they are, in their culture and space, and being church in new skins.

For instance, in England, there's "Messy Church," which is a fresh expression for families with kids: they meet in a hall for crafts, food, and a short worship time tailored to people who don't do "pews and sermons," and it's brought many non-church families to faith. In the U.S. and Australia, there are "dinner churches" where people gather around a meal each week, breaking bread much like the early disciples, sharing testimonies and a brief message. It's informal but deeply spiritual. A microchurch example: a group of college students starts a "campus coffee church," where they meet at a coffee shop, discuss Jesus over lattes, and that's their church community. Or consider a group of surfers in Brazil who start a beachside fellowship, where they surf together at dawn and then hold a Bible study and prayer on the sand. These are real examples.

Let me share an incredible story from a U.S. city. A young woman felt a burden for her neighborhood, where many people felt isolated and wouldn't be caught dead in a traditional church. She started a simple monthly gathering in her home called "Oikos" (meaning "family" in Greek).[89] They would invite neighbors for a potluck meal: no formal sermon, just eating together, sharing life stories, and maybe a short prayer

---

[89] Willesden, "A Fresh Expression of Church."

of thanks. Initially, it was just a few people, but it soon grew. They dubbed it "the church of the mundane" because it focused on finding God in everyday life through activities such as cooking, conversation, and mutual assistance.[90] One month, they asked, "What do our neighbors need?" They noticed some families struggled to pay for childcare, so Oikos organized free babysitting nights. Another time, they held a "free garage sale," collecting good-quality items and giving them away to anyone in need.[91] When a local single mother was evicted, one of the Oikos families took her and her children in for a few nights until they found shelter.[92] In essence, this little microchurch became the hands and feet of Jesus on that block: a spiritual family living out faith in very practical ways. People who had never been interested in church found themselves praying at that dinner table, experiencing love and community. Oikos eventually held informal worship nights, but the core was about doing life together with Jesus at the center. It was so outside the box that some traditional folks questioned, "Is that really a church?" But it was. As the organizer said, "Aren't God's people on mission in the church?"[93] They truly were a church for those neighbors.

Microchurches and fresh expressions are multiplying because they can reach niches and networks that traditional churches miss. There are biker churches for motorcycle enthusiasts, "cowboy churches" that meet in barns, skate park ministries for skateboarders, and even a "church in a pub" in one city, where people gather for spiritual discussions over a pint. Importantly, these aren't just Bible studies; they view themselves as authentic churches, offering community, discipleship, mission, and worship in innovative forms. Many are lay-led. In parts of Latin America and Asia, where resources are scarce, microchurches are a practical way to expand: there is no need for a formal building or a full-time pastor. These are just faithful leaders who open their homes.

---

90 Willesden, "A Fresh Expression of Church."
91 Willesden, "A Fresh Expression of Church."
92 Willesden, "A Fresh Expression of Church."
93 Willesden, "A Fresh Expression of Church."

For mission, this is gold. It means the church can pop up anywhere, in any cultural form that honors Christ. It makes the gospel accessible. People who might never dress up for Sunday service find that church can resemble a backyard barbecue, where Jesus is discussed around the fire pit. And these small units can also reproduce: each microchurch can inspire others. For example, the Tampa Underground Network in Florida began with a handful of microchurches; today, it's a network of over 200 microchurches reaching diverse subcultures, including hip-hop artists and homeless communities. Similarly, in the UK, fresh expressions have drawn tens of thousands of previously unchurched people into Christian community over the past 15 years. It shows us that the Holy Spirit is creative, not limited to one style of church. The message doesn't change, but the container can. As society changes, these new expressions are often at the forefront of mission. They remind us of the early church meeting in houses or the Wesleyan class meetings: small groups on mission. It's really a renewal of an old idea in a fresh context.

For the broader church, embracing microchurches and fresh expressions requires grace and flexibility: sometimes these groups don't look "orthodox" in form. Still, by focusing on discipleship and community, they bear real spiritual fruit. It's part of the church learning to "sing a new song" in mission. And it's very exciting because it means no one is unreachable: if someone won't come to church, well, the church (in micro form) can go to them.

Conclusion

Host: Wow, what an inspiring tour of how Christian mission is changing around the globe! We've heard about everything from online evangelists to house churches, environmental stewardship to reverse missionaries. These ten trends (digital outreach, migration and diaspora missions, reverse mission, local leadership, creation care, polycentric collaboration, integral mission, Spirit-empowered witness, rapid church planting movements, fresh expressions, and microchurches) paint a picture of a vibrant, ever-adapting global church.

Graham: It really is fantastic. The Holy Spirit is at work in so many ways. The gospel remains unchanging, but the methods of mission continue to evolve to reach people in each unique context. I hope that listeners are encouraged that God's mission is very much alive. Whether you're a student sharing Christ on social media, a businessperson welcoming immigrants in Jesus's name, or a pastor open to fresh expressions, you can be part of these global shifts. The core of the mission remains Jesus's Great Commission (to make disciples of all nations), and what we're seeing is God removing barriers and opening new avenues to do just that. It's an excellent time to be involved in God's work. As we've heard through these stories, one person's step of faith (whether starting a prayer on Facebook or hosting a dinner in their home) can literally save lives and transform communities.

Host: Do you have any final takeaway for our listeners?

Graham: I'd say, be open to change and creativity in how we spread the gospel. The message of Christ's love remains as powerful as ever, and these global trends demonstrate that when we step out in faith (whether through a smartphone, planting a tree, or starting a microchurch), God is present. The mission field might be right next door, online, or in a context you never expected. So pray, listen, and join what God is doing. That's what these changes are all about: reaching people where they are, in the language and form they understand. And God is faithfully honoring those efforts.

Host: Amen. Thank you so much for sharing these insights and stories. It's been eye-opening and heartening to hear how the church is crossing new frontiers. I'm sure our listeners are as encouraged as I'm to innovate in their own context and be part of God's mission.

Graham: Thank you. It's been a pleasure. God bless you all, and let's all continue to participate in what God is doing across the world.

Host: You've been listening to "Missions on the Move: Ten Global Shifts in Christian Mission." Thank you for tuning in. Until next time, may we all embrace the call to love God and love others in fresh and faithful ways.

8. Activism with a Monk's Heart: Thurman's Secret for Sustainable Justice

Righteous anger rises in the streets as protesters chant for justice. In the United States, Black Lives Matter rallies cry out against systemic racism. In Australia, voices lift for First Nations dignity and reconciliation. The church professes that it should be "no haven for racism" and that it must lead in justice, reconciliation, and healing; yet too often Sunday morning remains segregated, and believers splinter over questions of social activism.[94] In this tense and demanding environment, many faithful activists find themselves weary and wounded. Burnout stalks those who carry the burdens of racial injustice. How can the fire for justice be sustained without turning into the ashes of despair or hatred? Is there a deeper well from which to draw strength so that our pursuit of racial reconciliation remains bold and compassionate?

"How can the fire for justice be sustained without turning into the ashes of despair or hatred?"

Howard Thurman, a mystic mentor of the civil rights movement, offers a profound answer: Activism must be nourished by contemplation. The secret to sustainable justice, Thurman taught, is cultivating the heart of a monk even as we fight for what's right. His life and wisdom invite us to discover an inner sanctuary that empowers public resistance, enabling us to carry out activism with a monk's heart.

---

[94] McCracken, "21 Challenges Facing the 21st Century Church."

The Contemplative Soul of the Civil Rights Movement

In the midst of the Civil Rights era, as hoses blasted and hate raged, there was an often unseen source of strength sustaining the movement's leaders. It wasn't in the clamor, but in the quiet that their courage was renewed. Before marches in Alabama or freedom rides across the South, groups of activists would kneel, holding hands in prayer and singing hymns. One civil rights veteran recalled that without prayer, the movement would have been "like a bird without wings."[95] These women and men drew on spiritual resources beyond themselves. Their secret was a life of prayer beneath the life of protest. And behind many of them stood Howard Thurman, a spiritual guide who embodied contemplative nonviolence.

Thurman wasn't on the front lines shouting into megaphones or drafting policy demands. Instead, he was a pastoral presence and teacher of the deep spiritual life. An African American theologian born in 1899 under Jim Crow segregation, Thurman knew racial injustice intimately. Yet Thurman believed that real change required a transformation of the spirit, not just a change in laws. In 1936, he traveled to India and spent time with Mahatma Gandhi. Thurman resonated more with Gandhi's mystical center than with his political tactics.[96] He became convinced that the courage to resist evil nonviolently must flow from an encounter with the Divine. For Thurman, nonviolence was far more than a strategy: it was a way of being grounded in prayer.

Thurman went on to mentor generation-shaping leaders like Martin Luther King Jr., James Farmer, Vernon Jordan, and Jessie Jackson. Dr. King famously kept Thurman's book *Jesus and the Disinherited* with him as a spiritual guide. Thurman's influence helped

---

[95] In a 2004 PBS *Religion & Ethics NewsWeekly* interview, John Lewis said, "Without prayer, without faith in the Almighty, the civil rights movement would have been like a bird without wings." Interview by Kim Lawton. *"John Lewis Extended Interview."* The metaphor of "activism and contemplation as the two wings of a great bird of justice" originates from the teachings of Mahayana Buddhism, so I've modified that metaphor here.

[96] Werntz, "Howard Thurman's Contemplative Nonviolence."

King and others see that nonviolent resistance is unsustainable without an inner life of contemplation and love. The pastor-mystic taught them what he called "the strength beyond our strength," an inner power from God that could renew weary souls and keep hope alive when outer circumstances were crushing.[97] Thurman would urge activists to take regular "lulls in the rhythm of doing," pauses for prayer and reflection, knowing that without these sacred stops the relentless pace of justice work could derail them.[98] A community united across lines of difference, their solidarity was rooted in something more profound than a moment's passion.

"Their secret was a life of prayer beneath the life of protest."

Thurman's own life modeled this integration of action and contemplation. In 1944, he co-founded the church for the Fellowship of All Peoples in San Francisco: one of the first intentionally interracial congregations in the United States.[99] At a time when even churches were segregated, Thurman's congregation was a living proclamation that the walls of racism could be overcome through the Spirit of God. This "Fellowship Church" was devoted to, in Thurman's words, "personal empowerment and social transformation through an ever-deepening relationship with the Spirit of God in all life." Here's the blueprint Thurman offered: social transformation grows from spiritual transformation. He believed the church must become a courageous counter-community of reconciliation, a living model of God's justice. Policy changes and protests, he argued, wouldn't be enough if our souls remained captive to fear, hatred, and ego. So, Thurman remained a man of the chapel and classroom, nurturing the souls of activists so that their public witness sprang from a well of grace.

---

[97] Sanchez, "What We Can Learn from the Contemplative Heart."
[98] Sanchez, "What We Can Learn from the Contemplative Heart."
[99] Werntz, "Howard Thurman's Contemplative Nonviolence."

Centering Down: Finding an Inner Oasis

At the heart of Thurman's teaching is a practice he called "centering down." "How good it is to center down!"[100] Thurman wrote in a famous meditation. "To sit quietly and see one's self pass by!" This simple yet profound practice of stillness is a lifeline for those engaged in the long struggle for justice. When we "center down," we step away from the noise and chaos: not to escape reality, but to encounter a deeper Reality. Thurman described how our minds are like busy streets with endless traffic; our spirits are cluttered with clashing noises. But if we sit quietly and wait, a deeper note sounds beneath the turbulence. In the stillness, "there's a sound of another kind (a deeper note) which only the stillness of the heart makes clear." It's the voice of the Eternal, speaking in the depths of our being, offering "strength to weakness, courage to fear, hope to despair."[101]

For activists, this practice of silence and solitude isn't a luxury; it's a matter of survival. The work of racial justice can fill one's heart with righteous anger, frustration at the slow pace of change, and sorrow at each new injustice. Without an inner oasis, these feelings can harden into cynicism or consume us entirely. Thurman's invitation to center down is an invitation to return to the Source. It's in the secret place of prayer that we remember that God is God, and we aren't alone responsible for saving the world. We allow the "peace of the Eternal" to replenish us. In that contemplation, we face the hard questions: "What drives my activism? Is it centered in love or distorted by ego? What truly matters most?" Centering down recenters us on God's presence and purpose, so that when we return to the struggle, we carry a stillness within us.

"How good it is to center down! To sit quietly and see one's self pass by!" – Howard Thurman

---

100 Thurman, *Meditations of the Heart.*
101 Thurman, *Meditations of the Heart.*

Consider Jesus's example: Christ would withdraw to lonely places to pray at the height of ministry, then return empowered to heal and confront injustice. In one Gospel story, as a storm raged and his disciples panicked, Jesus slept peacefully in the boat. When he awoke, he calmed the storm with a word ("Peace, be still"), a prophetic authority flowing from inward stillness. Likewise, our prophetic action must flow from inner peace. Thurman knew this well. He taught that only the truly quiet heart can be a vessel of God's reconciling love in tumultuous times. The more ferocious the tempest of injustice, the more crucial it is for activists to carry a calm center within, anchored in prayer.

The Rhythm of Prayer and Protest

Modern activists often struggle with the balance between contemplation and action (I appreciate the way Richard Rohr integrates these in his ministry). In the face of urgent injustice, some worry that too much contemplation leads to passivity or "navel-gazing." On the other hand, relentless action without spiritual grounding leads to burnout, misguided rage, and even the risk of becoming what we resist. Thurman offers a "virtuous cycle" instead of a false choice. He challenges us that "those who'd be contemplative must identify with those who suffer, and those who'd address suffering must be contemplative."[102] In other words, prayer and protest are inextricably linked. Each fuels the other in a healthy rhythm.

Imagine activism and contemplation as the two wings of a great bird of justice: without one, we will never truly soar. When we pray deeply, we're driven to love and stand with the oppressed, because we have touched the heart of God who hears the cry of the poor. When we act for justice, we soon discover our need to return to prayer, to purify our motives and replenish our strength. Thurman witnessed this rhythm among the civil rights faithful. They'd pray before the march to center themselves in nonviolence and divine love. Then they'd march, sing,

---

[102] Werntz, "Howard Thurman's Contemplative Nonviolence."

suffer arrest or assault, and afterwards, they'd gather again to pray, forgive, and refill their souls with grace to continue. Action led them back to contemplation, which in turn prepared them for further action in an ongoing cycle. This "quiet strength," as some have called it, is the key to longevity in justice movements. Genuine peace and justice are born from recognizing our shared humanity.

"Imagine activism and contemplation as the two wings of a great bird of justice: without one, we'll never truly soar."

Thurman once told Martin Luther King Jr., after King endured a near-fatal stabbing, to extend his recovery and rest before returning to the fray. "Stand still so that you can continue to stand firm for justice," he advised.[103] King heeded that counsel, spending extra weeks in prayerful reflection. In that lull, King reportedly gained clarity and inner fortitude for the greater trials to come, believing that this forced pause was "part of God's plan to prepare him for larger work."[104] This illustrates a counterintuitive truth: sometimes the most critical act of faith is to stop and pray, trusting that being with God will ultimately empower us to do more effectively. In a culture that prizes ceaseless activism, Thurman's legacy reminds us that holy pause isn't paralysis, it's preparation. As he said, "There must be for me a deep sense of relatedness to God . . . This alone will make it possible for me to stand anything that life can or may do to me."[105]

When we embrace this rhythm of prayer and protest, we break the cycle of exhaustion. No longer is activism a frantic effort carried on our shoulders alone; it becomes a partnership with the Spirit. We act, then relinquish the results into God's hands in prayer. We speak boldly against injustice, then return to the silence to listen for the "still small voice" that corrects and consoles us. Over time, this rhythm carves out a vessel of

---

[103] Sanchez, "What We Can Learn from the Contemplative Heart."
[104] Sanchez, "What We Can Learn from the Contemplative Heart."
[105] Sanchez, "What We Can Learn from the Contemplative Heart."

peace in our hearts. We become, as Thurman envisioned, contemplatives in action: driven by love, not by restless anxiety or self-righteous anger.

Love at the Center of Protest

Perhaps the greatest gift a contemplative approach offers to activism is this: the capacity to love truly, even in the midst of protest. Racial justice work is inherently confrontational; it stands against oppressive systems and calls out prejudice. It's easy, even understandable, for those fighting racism to develop bitterness toward oppressors or those who remain complicit. Yet Thurman and other spiritual leaders in the freedom movements insisted that hatred can't drive out hatred; only love can. Nonviolence isn't merely the absence of physical violence; it's the presence of agapē love toward all, including one's adversaries. But how can activists possibly love their enemy when faced with bigotry, violence, and ignorance?

Thurman's answer: only through a transformed heart grounded in God. In the mystical encounter of prayer, as he taught, our ego (with its thirst for vindication and its tendency to dehumanize others) is dethroned. We see ourselves truthfully and repent of our own pride and hatred. We also come to see the sacred dignity in every person, even those who perpetrate injustice. Thurman wrote that Jesus rejected the way of hate because hatred destroys the hater and entrenches the cycle of violence.[106] Jesus, standing with his back against the wall of oppression, still chose to love and forgive, pointing a way out of endless vengeance. This radical love in action isn't natural to us; it's the fruit of the Spirit, cultivated by abiding in prayer.

"The activist with a monk's heart doesn't demonize individuals, even as they denounce unjust systems. Instead, they testify to the higher truth of our shared humanity under God."

---

[106] Thurman, *Jesus and the Disinherited.*

When activists integrate contemplation, they're better able to embody love in protest. This doesn't mean becoming timid or losing the prophetic edge: on the contrary, it infuses the fight for justice with divine power. Love gives moral courage that outlasts anger alone. A person centered in God's love can stare down hate with unflinching truth and compassion. Consider the posture of many civil rights marchers who, trained in nonviolence, met spit and slurs from white supremacists with songs and steady gazes that refused to return hate. That discipline was forged in churches, in prayer meetings, in hours of inner work. As Thurman put it, through prayer, "our false selves are undone," and we're enabled to see even our oppressor through God's eyes. The activist with a monk's heart doesn't demonize individuals, even as they denounce unjust systems. Instead, they testify to the higher truth of our shared humanity under God. Their protest is aimed not at revenge but at redemption: seeking to free both the oppressed and the oppressor from the dehumanization of racism.

Such spiritually-rooted love has transformative potential. We have accounts of white segregationists whose hearts were softened by the dignified suffering love of Black protesters. We see contemporary examples: protesters kneeling in prayer for those who persecute them, or families of victims extending words of forgiveness that confound the world. These are miracles of grace in the public square, and they arise from deep wells of faith. Activism informed by contemplation resists the temptation to mirror the world's rage and division. Instead, it stands apart with a peculiar power: the power of unyielding love. This is how the church can truly be a light in dark times: by producing activists who carry the presence of Christ into the streets, who do justice with mercy and humility (Micah 6:8). In such hearts, there's no haven for racism, because the love of God melts prejudice.

Practices for the Contemplative Activist

How can we cultivate this integration of zeal and peace, of justice-making and soul-keeping? In practical terms, what might it look like to engage in activism with a monk's heart? Here are some concrete spiritual practices and approaches:

- Daily "Centering Down": Set aside time each day for silent prayer, meditation, or centering prayer. Even ten or twenty minutes of intentional silence (perhaps in the morning before work or activism) can center your spirit. In that quiet, breathe deeply and acknowledge God's presence. Let your anxious thoughts pass by. Listen for that "deeper note" of the Spirit. This daily practice will ground your activism in something more profound than news cycles and give you inner steadiness amid chaos.

- Sabbath and Regular Retreats: Honor the rhythm of work and rest that God ordained. Take a Sabbath day each week where you step back from activism, social media, and news. Use that time for worship, family, nature, and things that renew you. Additionally, consider occasional retreats, such as a weekend at a retreat center or a day of solitude in a peaceful location. As Thurman advised King, standing still for a season can prepare you to stand firm later. These larger pauses will replenish your vision and prevent burnout by reconnecting you with the joy of simply being beloved of God, apart from your work.

- Prayer Partners and Communities: Don't walk the contemplative path alone. Find fellow sojourners who value prayer as the driving force behind their actions. This might mean forming a small prayer group within your activist circle or joining a contemplative prayer gathering at your church. Before heading out to a protest or strategy meeting, gather for prayer. Sing a hymn or spiritual song together to unite your spirits. Encourage one another to seek God's face. The early civil rights movement was sustained by church communities that prayed and worshipped fiercely, generating a collective resilience. Community prayer keeps each person accountable to love and bolsters courage through mutual support.

- Sacramental Rituals in Activism: Integrate symbolic acts of faith into your activism. For example, some protestors have incorporated kneeling in prayer or moments of silence during demonstrations. Others carry a cross or light candles at vigils for victims of racial violence. These acts remind everyone present that the struggle for justice is ultimately a spiritual struggle, and they invite God's presence into the public square. Be creative in incorporating rituals of lament, confession, and hope into your justice work. Such practices can turn a rally into holy ground and a march into a moving liturgy for change.

- Lectio Divina and Sacred Study: Nourish your mind and heart with wisdom from Scripture and spiritual writings. Practice lectio divina (the slow, prayerful reading of Scripture) focusing on passages about God's heart for justice, mercy, and reconciliation. Meditate on the prophets or the Gospels where Jesus ministers to the marginalized. Also read the writings of contemplative leaders and justice seekers, including the mystics, the saints, and modern prophets of nonviolence. Howard Thurman's own works, like Meditations of the Heart or Jesus and the Disinherited, are rich resources to study. Allow these readings to read you, to search your soul and reshape your perspectives. Continual formation through sacred study ensures that your activism remains theologically rooted and spiritually attuned.

- Examen of Activism: At the end of each day or week, perform an examen: a review of your life in the light of God's presence. Specifically, examine your activism and relationships across racial lines. Where did you feel most aligned with God's love and purpose in your work? Where did you feel anxiety, anger, or ego creeping in? Gently review moments of conflict or discouragement: do you need to forgive someone, or seek forgiveness? Are you harboring resentment that needs to be released? Offer it all to God and ask for guidance to grow in love. This regular examen keeps your soul free of the bitter residues that often accompany justice work, ensuring you can continue with a pure heart.

- Embodied Contemplative Practices: Remember that contemplation isn't only sitting silently: it can also be embodied. Practices such as walking meditation, yoga, sacred dance, or simply mindful breathing can help integrate body and spirit. Perhaps, before a difficult community meeting, you take a slow prayer walk around the block, repeating a simple mantra, such as "Your peace, O God," with each step. Some activists find solace in music or art as a form of prayer: singing a soulful hymn, drumming in a circle, or expressing their emotions through painting. Find the practices that settle your body and focus your mind on the divine. A calm body supports a calm spirit, and both are needed when tensions flare on the justice journey.

Each person's blend of practices will differ; the key is intentionality and consistency. The monk's heart isn't formed in a day: it's the fruit of daily tending. Over time, you may notice that you carry a deep sense of God's presence even in stressful strategy debates or while reading the day's grim headlines. You may react less out of reactivity and more out of a rooted compassion. This is the transformation Thurman spoke of ("our transformation goes all the way down to our bones"), making us people who can, as he said, "embody the way of Jesus, chastened in prayer and quieted in our anger, steeled with a moral courage that no violence can efface."

Conclusion: Leading with a New Spirit

The challenges of racial injustice in our time are formidable. In the United States and parts of Europe, a resurgence of overt racism and nationalism tests the progress of past decades. In Australia, the ongoing work of truth-telling and reconciliation with Indigenous peoples calls for courage and humility. The church, if it's to answer its call to be an ambassador of reconciliation, must itself undergo this deep integration of contemplation and action. Churches are invited to become training grounds for contemplative activists: nurturing believers in spiritual disciplines that fortify them to confront injustice in society. There can be no haven for racism in our congregations, and likewise no haven for apathy or despair. Empowered by prayer, the people of God can move out of comfort zones and into the hard places of suffering with a love that sustains.

Activism with a monk's heart isn't easy, but it's essential for the long haul. We do this because ultimately, racial reconciliation is God's work before it's ours. We're participants in God's healing mission, and we can't do it apart from God's life flowing through us. Howard Thurman's legacy whispers to this generation of activists: Slow down. Center down. Seek the Face of the Eternal. Let God's love renew your mind and purge your soul of bitterness. Let holy silence teach you who you are and who your neighbor is in God's sight. Then, with that monk-like heart burning with divine fire, rise and go into the streets. Speak truth, do justice, confront evil: but do it as a bearer of peace that passes understanding.

Sustainable justice is about more than winning policy or cultural battles; it's about becoming the Beloved Community we proclaim. It means living the unity and equity we long for, through the Spirit's power. With contemplation joined to activism, we can press on without burning out, because our source is inexhaustible. We will find ourselves part of a virtuous cycle of grace: prayer fueling action, and action driving us back to prayer. And in that faithful rhythm, by God's grace, the long arc of the moral universe bends a little more toward justice: through our hands and hearts, steadied by the Eternal Love that makes all things new.[107]

---

[107] King, *"Remaining Awake Through a Great Revolution."*

9. Four Qualities of Missional Movements Born at the Margins

Missional movements are born at the margins. They thrive there. And they spread out from there. God doesn't only place the margins at the center of his love, concern, and mission. God begins movements there.

God's mission is from the margins. Jesus was a Galilean Jew. He didn't just care for the margins: He was from the margins himself. If the church's mission, ministry, and message are to reflect the way that God places the margins at the center of his love and concern, then the church must see the margins as not merely being incidental to the whole.

Jayakumar Christian spoke at the launch of my book *World Christianity: An Introduction* (the first edition was called *Global Church*).[108] Jayakumar Christian served as the Partnership Director for Faith and Development at World Vision International. He's based in Chennai, India.

At the book launch, Jayakumar Christian offered four qualities of missional movements born at the margins.

Mission Must Disrupt and Disturb the Status Quo

Mission is about challenging the usual questions that are asked and raising disruptive questions.

In God's "upside-down kingdom," Jesus confronts the god-complexes of the rich, powerful, influential, connected, and religious. And he births missional movements at the margins, among the poor,

---

[108] Hill, *World Christianity.*

weak, rejected, discriminated-against, discarded, powerless, and "unclean."

Missional movements challenge and redefine power. Jesus reveals a kingdom where the god-complexes of the world (most commonly enjoyed by the rich and powerful, as wealth and power often tempt us to play god in the lives of others) are exposed for what they truly are: illusions, distortions, and lies.

Mission born at the margins confronts our god-complexes. It calls them out for what they really are. In such a mission, Jesus demands repentance and dependence on the one true God. He reveals himself in the weakest and most unexpected places and among the most unlikely people. And he calls us to use what power, privilege, wealth, and status we have to enrich others, care for those most vulnerable, address injustice, usher in peace, and support human flourishing.

If our mission isn't disturbing and disrupting the status quo, then there's a problem.

Mission born at the margins challenges the usual questions and their religious and power-based assumptions. It asks disruptive and disturbing questions about religion, wealth, identity, national pride, race and gender relations, power, and more.

Jesus disturbs and disrupts the comfortable status quo. And in missional movements, he reveals that he's present among the margins and moving from there. He invites us to confront the status quo and offer an alternative.

Mission is about Holiness that's Relational and Inclusive

Mission is about washing feet and embracing others. It's about my life and your life: whole faith matters, character matters, spirituality matters: these things are primary, not programs and strategies.

Too often, our mission and church life are characterized by a piety that excludes and builds walls between people. In self-righteous exclusivity, we shut people out of our communities unless they conform, "shape up," or mirror our dysfunctional religiosity.

But mission born at the margins reveals a holiness that's relational and inclusive. It shows a commitment to salvation through reconciliation, peacemaking, and embracing. The reconciliatory spirit of salvation holds unique possibilities for human interaction and peace. He's our peace, who has broken down all walls of enmity and division. Acts of God's love form us as human beings, bring us into community, reconcile us to others, and recreate the world.

The church needs a missiology of embrace, especially in relationship to the despised and the vulnerable.

Mission born at the margins shows us that freedom from hatred and indifference towards others comes by engaging them as whole human beings. They're persons created in God's image. They're people for whom Christ has died. They're people who have been called and destined for future glory. We must situate the "other" person in the grand narrative of Scripture, and, consequently, embrace them.

Embracing the "other" isn't about abandoning truth or the gospel. But it's about embracing people while respecting their distinctive cultures, views, histories, and futures. The Cross is a symbol of overcoming enmity. The Cross is a symbol of coming to fellowship with those who have been estranged. It isn't easy to open oneself up to the other in a posture of embrace. But the Spirit enables these counter-cultural, kingdom-based acts.

Christianity is a faith symbolized by the basin and the towel. It's the faith of the reconciling Cross. Mission is about holiness demonstrated through acts of service, such as washing feet and embracing others.

Mission Movements Create Ripples of Transformation

Missional movements are born at the margins; monuments are built at the center. Movements often occur when we choose intentional powerlessness: relinquishing power and control and depending on the Spirit of Christ.

Jesus shapes movements that cause "ripples of transformation. A prophetic community must evolve into a movement. Sporadic examples of excellence won't sustain change. Movements are critical. Movements are rooted in neighborhoods. The prophetic community must be incarnated in the neighborhood; otherwise, its work would be mere activism. Solutions for a transformative movement affecting the nation should be molded, tested, and shaped in the neighborhood."[109]

Missional movements are incarnational, cruciform, weak, and ethical movements. They're movements of and from the margins. They create surprising, unstoppable ripples of transformation.

Missional Being Precedes Missional Doing

Mission is about being in Christ. Mission born at the margins shows us that missional being always precedes missional doing. More than that: Missional spirituality and missional activity must be inextricable.

My being matters, and my relationship with Christ matters. Only life reproduces life. Programs don't. In mission, whole-of-life spirituality and character matter.

Jayakumar Christian says that the church needs a spirituality of dirt and dust. David Bosch refers to this as a spirituality of the road.

Christian spirituality and discipleship grow in mission. They resource mission. They're inseparable from mission. They're the oxygen for mission. They need mission to flourish. David Bosch says we don't have to choose between spirituality and mission.

"Spirituality isn't contemplation over against action. It's not a flight from the world over against involvement in the world . . . Involvement in this world should lead to a deepening of our relationship with and dependence on God, and the deepening of this relationship should, in turn, lead to an increasing involvement in the world. Pouring

---

[109] Christian, "Rise of the Urban Poor," in Hill, ed., *Signs of Hope in the City*, 23.

out our love on people in selfless dedication is a form of prayer . . . Spirituality is all-pervading."[110]

Spirituality, discipleship, and mission are inextricable. There's no true mission without discipleship. And there's no authentic discipleship without mission.

A spirituality of missional engagement means that missional being precedes missional doing. A spirituality of missional engagement means that worship, community, discipleship, and mission are inextricably linked.

Jayakumar Christian offers four qualities of missional movements born at the margins: Mission must disturb and disrupt the status quo. Mission is about holiness that is relational and inclusive. Mission movements create ripples of transformation. And missional being precedes missional doing.

---

[110] Bosch, *A Spirituality of the Road*, 13–14.

PART III—HEALING THE SOUL OF THE PUBLIC SQUARE

Part 3 turns from critique to constructive vision: exploring how faith can renew civic life, imagination, and hope amid ideological exhaustion and polarization.

10. Pulling Back from the Brink: A Spiritual Path Beyond Toxic Politics

The air feels charged with anger. Outrage spreads like fire through our feeds. Families split across political lines, friends grow suspicious, neighbors draw the curtains. In many Western nations, democracy itself groans under the weight of distrust, misinformation, and division.[111] Political culture has become toxic, not only in what leaders say, but in what ordinary citizens begin to breathe, absorb, and repeat.

Yet underneath the noise, the majority longs for another way. Many are weary of living on the edge of constant outrage, of choosing sides like teams in a war, of assuming the worst of those who differ. A hunger rises for a different spirit: one that pulls us back from the brink, restores civil discourse, renews democracy, and rebuilds the fragile common good.

The question is urgent: how do we find the off-ramp? How do we step away from the cliff edge and turn toward life again?

When Politics Turns Deadly

We don't need more evidence that our political culture has crossed a dangerous threshold, yet it keeps arriving.[112] The murder of Charlie Kirk, no matter one's politics, is a wound to the whole body. It joins a grim list: elected officials attacked in their homes, legislators harassed on the streets, staffers threatened, judges and election workers living under

---

[111] Levendusky, *How Partisan Media Polarize America.*
[112] Levitsky and Ziblatt, *How Democracies Die.*

constant fear. What was once unthinkable has become tragically familiar: political disagreement giving way to intimidation, hatred, and even bloodshed.

When political opponents become enemies to be eliminated rather than neighbors to be argued with, democracy collapses under the weight of fear. When fear rules, truth is silenced, mercy withers, and every policy dispute carries the shadow of violence. The danger isn't only to public servants but to the soul of the people.

The Christian vision insists that no neighbor can be reduced to an enemy without also reducing ourselves. The cross of Christ exposes violence as a lie, a counterfeit solution that leaves only ruin. And it summons us to another way: to see even adversaries as bearers of dignity, to wrestle with ideas rather than destroy those who hold them, to create space for robust disagreement without surrendering to rage.

We must lament every act of political violence. We must name it as sin, resist its normalization, and call forth communities of courage where words replace weapons and reconciliation outshines revenge. Only then will we find the off-ramp from this spiral of destruction.

A Prayer of Lament and Resolve

O God of peace,
we grieve the blood that has been spilled on our streets,
the voices silenced by hatred,
the leaders struck down by rage.
We confess our complicity in a culture that feeds division,
that prizes victory over truth,
that forgets the image of your love in every neighbor.
Hold before us the faces of those lost,
the families who mourn,
the communities shaken.
Don't let us grow numb to this sorrow.
Teach us again the ways of mercy,
the courage to speak truth without violence,

the patience to seek justice without vengeance,
the hope to build a common life where weapons are laid down
and words become tools of healing.
Through the cross of Christ,
reconcile what hatred has torn apart,
and make us instruments of your peace.
Amen.

Naming the Disease

To find healing, we must name the wound. Political polarization has turned difference into enmity. Debate has hardened into contempt. Outrage has become currency, cynicism a badge of honor. We live in a culture where scoring points matters more than seeking truth, and humiliating opponents is valued more than persuading them.

"When we no longer see the image of God in those across the aisle, democracy decays, and our humanity falters."

Violence hovers at the margins, sometimes spilling into the open. We see threats against leaders, hatred directed at neighbors, and ideologies clothed in religious garments that betray the very faith they claim. Social media amplifies the worst, rewarding extremity and reducing complex realities into slogans that wound rather than heal.

This isn't just politics; it's a spiritual crisis. When we no longer see the image of God in those across the aisle, democracy decays, and our humanity falters. When contempt replaces compassion, society begins to fracture at its very core.

The Spiritual Roots of Democracy

Democracy isn't only a political arrangement; it's a spiritual practice. At its heart lies the conviction that every person bears sacred worth, that voices should be heard, that power must be shared. Democracy presupposes humility: that no single group or party possesses the whole truth, and that we need one another to approximate wisdom.

"Democracy is a spiritual practice not merely a political arrangement."

The prophets of old spoke of justice rolling down like waters and righteousness like an ever-flowing stream (Amos 5:24). They reminded rulers and people alike that authority is a trust, and governance must serve the vulnerable. Jesus embodied a kingdom not of domination but of service, where the greatest are those who wash feet (John 13:12–15). These aren't just religious ideals; they are the spiritual soil out of which democracy grows.

When politics becomes toxic, it isn't simply a failure of policy but a betrayal of this sacred trust. To heal democracy, we must tend to the soul of our public life.

The Hunger for a Different Spirit

Beneath the shouting, most people are tired of living in a state of constant conflict. They want leaders who speak truth without venom, who can disagree without destroying, who value cooperation over conquest. They want to see neighbors as neighbors again, not as enemies.

This longing is itself a grace. It's the Spirit groaning within societies that are weary of hatred. It's the holy discontent that says, "This isn't who you're meant to be."

The off-ramp begins here: in listening to this yearning, in trusting that the vast majority doesn't want to live at war, in believing that renewal is possible.

"The off-ramp begins here: in listening to this yearning, in trusting that the vast majority doesn't want to live at war, in believing that renewal is possible."

Practices for Pulling Back from the Brink

How then do we begin? Not with quick fixes, but with slow, deliberate practices that form a new political spirituality.

1. Practicing the Presence in Public Life

Mystics speak of practicing the presence of God in all things. What if we learned to practice presence in our politics? Before speaking, pause. Before posting, breathe. Before debating, remember the humanity of the one who differs. Carry into civic life the same reverence we bring to prayer, seeing opponents not as obstacles but as sacred icons of divine image.

> *"Carry into civic life the same reverence we bring to prayer, seeing opponents not as obstacles but as sacred icons of divine image."*

2. Choosing Curiosity Over Contempt

Contempt dehumanizes; curiosity dignifies. To ask, "Help me understand why you see it that way," is to resist the poison of polarization. It doesn't mean surrendering convictions but approaching difference with humility. Curiosity opens space for grace to move, even when agreement never comes.

3. Recovering Silence and Slowness

Toxic politics thrives on immediacy. Outrage demands instant reaction. But democracy requires patience. The contemplative path teaches us to slow down, to sit in silence, to listen deeply. If we can't be silent in prayer, we can't be calm in debate. Slowness restores proportion and gives wisdom room to speak.

4. Practicing Confession and Repentance

Each side of the political divide carries blame. Confession is the courage to admit complicity. Repentance is the willingness to change course. Without confession, we remain trapped in cycles of blame; with it, we open the door to renewal. Communities that confess together can also heal together.

"Without confession, we remain trapped in cycles of blame; with it, we open the door to renewal."

5. Re-Centering on the Common Good

The prophets remind us that proper governance seeks justice for those experiencing poverty, liberation for the oppressed, and dignity for the forgotten. When politics is reduced to tribal gain, the common good disappears. To restore democracy is to recover the vision of shared flourishing: that my neighbor's well-being is bound up with mine.

The Role of the Church and Communities of Faith

If democracy is to be renewed, communities of faith must reclaim their prophetic vocation. Not as chaplains to parties, but as witnesses to the kingdom that transcends them all. Not as cheerleaders for ideologies, but as servants of truth, reconciliation, and justice.

The church should be the one place where people of different views can pray together, eat together, and work for the good of the world together. It should be a community where we learn how to hold differences without division, how to speak the truth in love, and how to embody the reconciling Christ in a fractured age.

"When the church baptizes partisan rage, it betrays the gospel. But when it models humility, compassion, and courage, it becomes a sanctuary for hope."

When the church baptizes partisan rage, it betrays the gospel. But when it models humility, compassion, and courage, it becomes a sanctuary for hope.

Prophetic Resistance to Violence and Lies

Pulling back from the brink doesn't mean softening truth or ignoring injustice. The contemplative life gives us courage to resist lies, name violence, and stand against oppression. But it teaches us to do so without hatred, without mirroring the tactics of those we oppose.

The cross is the ultimate act of resistance and reconciliation: absorbing violence without returning it, exposing lies without becoming a liar, defeating death through the surrender of love. To follow the crucified One in political life is to resist with both courage and compassion.

Reimagining Disagreement

What if disagreement were no longer a threat but a gift? In a democracy, disagreement isn't failure; it's the way wisdom emerges. When handled with respect, disagreement sharpens thought, broadens vision, and protects against tyranny.

To reimagine disagreement is to remember that unity isn't uniformity, and peace isn't silence. It's possible to disagree robustly while still affirming the dignity of those across the table. This is the discipline we must relearn if democracy is to survive.

Stories of Renewal

Throughout history, societies have found ways to escape despair and off-ramps from political violence. Nations scarred by war have chosen reconciliation. Leaders who were once at odds have forged bipartisan alliances for the sake of the vulnerable. Communities fractured by hatred have rediscovered common humanity in the rubble of disaster.

These stories remind us that the brink isn't the end. It's the place where repentance can begin, where mercy can surprise, where grace can interrupt the spiral of destruction.

A Mystical Vision for Public Life

Mystics teach us to see the world as charged with the presence of God. Imagine politics charged with that same awareness. Imagine debates carried out as if the Spirit hovered over them. Imagine policies shaped by prayerful listening, legislation born of humility, leaders formed in silence before they speak in public.

This mystical vision doesn't remove conflict, but it transforms its spirit. Politics becomes not a battlefield but a pilgrimage, not a zero-sum game but a shared journey toward justice.

The Hope Beyond Despair

It's easy to despair when violence erupts, when lies spread, when civility crumbles. But despair is itself a toxin, paralyzing the will to act. Hope isn't naïve optimism; it's stubborn trust that the Spirit is still at work, that resurrection follows crucifixion, that even now renewal is possible.

"Hope is stubborn trust that the Spirit is still at work, that resurrection follows crucifixion, that even now renewal is possible."

Hope looks at a polarized society and sees seeds of grace: ordinary neighbors longing for peace, quiet majorities who want something different, communities where reconciliation is being practiced in small but powerful ways. Hope dares to believe that the toxic spirit isn't the final word.

Stepping Off the Brink

We stand at a precipice. The culture of outrage tempts us to leap into chaos. But there is another way. There is an off-ramp, a path back to sanity and grace. It will require humility, silence, confession, curiosity, and courage. It will require communities of faith to model reconciliation, citizens to choose compassion over contempt, and leaders to put the common good above partisan gain.

This isn't easy. It's the way of the cross: costly, slow, and often misunderstood. But it's the only way that leads to life.

If we dare to walk this path, we may yet find ourselves surprised. We may discover that enemies can become neighbors again, that democracy can be healed, that truth and mercy can kiss in the public square. We may find that the brink wasn't the end, but the threshold of a new beginning.

And in that discovery, we'll glimpse the more profound truth: that politics, when purified, can become a form of love: an imperfect but real participation in the covenant of God, who calls us to seek justice, love mercy, and walk humbly in this world (Micah 6:8).

"Politics, when purified, when carried out as an expression of our discipleship to Christ, can become a form of love: an imperfect but real participation in the covenant of God."

11. Christ Without a Flag: Following Jesus in an Age of Christian Nationalism

Christian nationalism is the great confusion of our age. It fuses the cross and the flag, the gospel and the state, and the kingdom of God and the kingdoms of this world.[113] Christian nationalism takes the beauty of the faith and dresses it in the armor of empire. It baptizes political platforms as if they were gospels, blesses borders as if they were sacraments, and treats the nation as the chosen people while forgetting the wild, borderless kingdom that Jesus demonstrated and proclaimed.[114]

Here's my definition of Christian nationalism:

"Christian nationalism is a political and religious ideology that seeks to fuse a specific version of Christianity with the identity, history, laws, and culture of a nation, often promoting the idea that the state should privilege that faith and its adherents above others. Christian nationalism blends a narrow cultural identity with a selective form of Christianity, employing religious imagery and language to justify the pursuit of authority, influence, and dominance in civic life."

More concisely,

"Christian nationalism weds a narrow cultural identity to a selective Christianity and a specific brand of politics, using faith and its symbols to claim power, shape laws, control institutions, and privilege one group above others."

In the Sermon on the Mount, Jesus invites us into a reality that subverts every empire: a community of the poor in spirit, the merciful,

---

113 Whitehead and Perry, *Taking America Back for God.*
114 Gorski & Perry, *The Flag and the Cross*; Cavanaugh, *Migrations of the Holy.*

the peacemakers, and the persecuted for righteousness' sake.[115] He didn't name any earthly nations, empires, political rulers, borders, flags, exceptionalisms, or walls. Jesus flew no flag.

Christian nationalism opposes the gospel, kingdom, and way of Jesus Christ. Here's why:

"Christian nationalism opposes the gospel, kingdom, and way of Jesus Christ. The gospel of Jesus centers on self-giving love, humility, justice, and welcome for all, while Christian nationalism seeks power, control, and privilege for one group at the expense of others."

Christ's kingdom isn't defended by weapons but by wounds.

Christ's kingdom isn't extended by might and power but by . . .

> praying before dawn,
>
> caring for the stranger at the door,
>
> sharing bread with the hungry,
>
> seeing the image of God in every face,
>
> setting chairs for enemies to sit and eat,
>
> breaking snares, so people are freed,
>
> repairing what's been shattered,
>
> acting to confront injustice,
>
> and creating places of refuge for the weary.

Jesus's kingdom isn't upheld by borders but by bread,

> not by marching but by mercy,
>
> not by conquest but by compassion,
>
> not by fear but by feast,
>
> not by siege but by song,
>
> not by might but by meekness,
>
> not by power but by peace,
>
> not by hate but by hospitality,
>
> not by force but by forgiveness,
>
> and not by exclusion but by embrace.

---

[115] Wright, *How God Became King.*

Christ's kingdom isn't revealed by battalions but by benedictions,

> not by rifles but by ripples of grace,
> not by sanctions but by sanctuaries,
> not by drones but by doxologies,
> not by slogans but by service,
> not by decrees but by deeds of love,
> not by crowns but by cross-bearing,
> not by boots but by blessings,
> not by fearmongering but by faithfulness,
> and not by domination but by divine self-giving.

"At the foot of the cross, there are no flags. There are only wounds."

To follow Christ is to live with an allegiance that relativizes every other loyalty. Jesus Christ is our Lord, and no other ruler or master can command our full allegiance. Every time an earthly ruler does something that contradicts the ethics and way of our Lord Jesus Christ, we must choose to follow Jesus regardless of the cost. Christian spirituality isn't apolitical, but it's never partisan in the ways the world demands. Discipleship to Jesus is rooted in a kingdom that refuses to be co-opted by nationalist fervor.

The Cross as a Rebuke to Power

The crucifixion is the definitive rebuke to the myth that God's purposes advance through coercive power.[116] Jesus was executed by a collaboration between religion and empire, a conspiracy between priests and politicians. They saw him as a threat because his kingdom would not bow to their control.

Christian nationalism in any form, whether draped in red, white, and blue or bearing other colors, makes the same mistake as those who crucified Christ: it assumes that God's will can be realized through dominance, force, and political supremacy. It forgets that the cross isn't

---

[116] Hauerwas, *Resident Aliens*; Miller, *The Religion of American Greatness.*

a symbol of victory by violence but of love poured out in suffering service.

The Christian mystical tradition reminds us that the path of Christ isn't one of upward mobility, but rather a downward descent. The one who could command legions of angels chose instead to be stripped, humiliated, and crucified. This wasn't weakness. It was the deepest expression of divine strength. Jesus revealed a God to us who is vulnerable, compassionate, and concerned for all humanity, while willing to confront empires, institutions, ideologies, and rulers with courage, ferocity, and unflinching loyalty to God and the kingdom of heaven. In doing so, Jesus set an example for us to follow. Following the way of Jesus, Christians reject allegiance to the world's rulers and nations and, instead, obey, serve, and give our full allegiance and loyalty to Christ alone, regardless of the cost. This makes Christians dangerous to personalities, institutions, and systems that demand allegiance and absolute power.

The resurrection that followed didn't vindicate the sword but the scars. It wasn't a triumph of political revolution but of life breaking through death, of a reign built on forgiveness rather than fear. Any movement that weds faith to national power misreads the story and mistakes the source of true authority.

To follow the crucified and risen Christ is to renounce every idol that demands allegiance at the expense of love. It means choosing service over status, welcome over walls, and truth over propaganda. The kingdom of God comes not through legislated piety but through lives laid down in costly, cruciform love.

"The crucified Christ isn't the mascot of empire. Christ is the outsider, the stranger, the one rejected by both religion and state."

The Temptation of the Nations

From the wilderness to Golgotha, Jesus was tempted with the kingdoms of the world. "All these I will give you," the adversary whispered, "if you will bow down." It was the promise of instant influence without the cross, of glory without the wounds. Jesus refused.

Christian nationalism is the old temptation in new clothes, the promise that if we align closely enough with political power, we can secure the world for God.[117] However, this path always leads to compromise and idolatry.

The contemplative life teaches us to recognize false consolations. It strips away illusions until all that is left is God. It invites us to resist the seduction of control and to live in the strange freedom of those whose citizenship is in heaven. Our hope isn't in seizing power but in embodying Christ's love, even when it costs us.

Nations and their political systems and personalities would like us to believe that morals, righteousness, and justice can be legislated into existence. Legal and political instrument have their place. However, holiness and love aren't the fruit of statecraft or legislation but of hearts transformed by grace, aligned to Christ, and empowered by the Holy Spirit. No political program can manufacture this.

When disciples of Jesus relinquish their call to follow Christ and, instead, wed themselves to political dominance, we risk trading our prophetic voice for a seat at the table of the Caesar, the Prime Minister, or the President. Yet, the gospel of Jesus Christ calls us not to rule from thrones, tanks, jets, or parliaments, but to wash feet in the places where power rarely stoops to serve.

Nationalism's Shrinking God

Nationalism, including its Christianized form, shrinks God to the size of a single nation's borders and values. It treats God as a tribal deity, bound to one people, one history, one culture. It elevates the nation as the

---

117 McKnight, *Kingdom Conspiracy.*

ultimate good, often at the expense of the vulnerable, the stranger, and the enemy.

But the God revealed in Christ is never parochial. This God loves Samaritans and Syrians, tax collectors and zealots, Romans and Judeans, citizens and undocumented immigrants, refugees and residents, prisoners and guards, the powerful and the powerless, the decadent dining in palaces and those experiencing poverty begging at their gates, the healthy and the sick, the devout and the doubting, the insider and the outcast, the neighbor next door and the stranger across the sea, those who welcome and those who resist, those who bless and those who curse, and those at the center of culture and those marginalized.

The early church was a borderless movement, scandalous in its refusal to divide Jew from Gentile, enslaved person from free, and male from female. These early disciples of Jesus called him *Kyrios* ("Lord"), knowing full well that Caesar claimed the same title. To confess Christ as Lord is to dethrone every nationalist claim to ultimate loyalty.

The True Gospel of Jesus Christ vs the False "Gospel" of Christian Nationalism

Christian spirituality doesn't merely critique nationalism. It laments the harm it causes. It grieves when faith is used to justify exclusion, when Scripture is weaponized against the stranger, when the symbols of faith are used to justify oppressing people and committing abuses, and when the cross is displayed alongside instruments of violence.

We must lament the way Christian nationalism distorts the gospel, turning it into a cultural badge rather than a summons to discipleship. We must name the injustice it perpetuates: racism, xenophobia, militarism, and economic exploitation cloaked in religious rhetoric.

The gospel of Jesus Christ isn't the same as the "gospel" of Christian nationalism. The gospel of Jesus Christ is the good news that the Creator has entered human history in the person of Jesus to reconcile all creation through his life, death, and resurrection. It proclaims that God's reign is breaking in, marked by forgiveness, liberation, justice, healing, and the restoration of all things. In this kingdom, the last are first, enemies are loved, the poor are blessed, and peace is made through self-giving love. It's a kingdom not of this world's systems, where power is redefined through the cross and life emerges from the empty tomb. This gospel calls all to repentance, faith, and discipleship in the way of Christ, embodying the values of God's reign here and now.

In contrast, the "gospel" of Christian nationalism is a political vision that fuses national identity with a particular expression of Christian faith. It claims that the security, moral health, and future of the nation depend on preserving its "Christian" character through political dominance, cultural control, and alignment of church with state. It tends to define faith in terms of protecting borders, preserving cultural traditions, securing influence, and wielding power to legislate morality. In this vision, loyalty to the nation is often intertwined with loyalty to God, and political victories are seen as spiritual triumphs.

Comparing and Contrasting Christ's True Gospel and Christian Nationalism's False "Gospel"

Gospel of Jesus Christ	"Gospel" of Christian Nationalism
Rooted in God's kingdom, which transcends national, ethnic, and cultural boundaries.	Rooted in a particular nation's identity, history, and political power.
Advances through sacrificial love, service, and humility.	Advances through political control, cultural dominance, and coercion.
Welcomes the stranger, loves enemies, and includes the marginalized.	Often prioritizes insiders, national loyalty, and cultural conformity.
Measures faithfulness by alignment with the way of the cross.	Measures faithfulness by alignment with political or national goals.
Seeks transformation of hearts and communities by the Spirit.	Seeks preservation of "Christian" cultural influence through legislation and power.
Finds hope in the resurrection and God's promised renewal of all things.	Finds hope in securing and defending a certain political and cultural order.
Defines victory as lives restored, enemies reconciled, and justice rolling down.	Defines victory as political wins, cultural dominance, and national security.

We must never trade the true gospel of Jesus Christ for the false "gospel" of Christian nationalism. The gospel of Jesus Christ calls us to die to self, take up the cross, and follow a king whose reign isn't of this world. The "gospel" of Christian nationalism calls people to defend and advance their nation as though it were the kingdom of God, often replacing the cruciform path with the pursuit of earthly power.

"The gospel isn't the property of any nation. It's the scandalous good news that the last will be first, the humble will be lifted, and the meek will inherit the earth."

Hospitality as Resistance

The cruciform way resists nationalism by practicing hospitality. In a culture of suspicion toward outsiders, the follower of Jesus opens the door. In a system that privileges the native-born, the Christian embraces the foreigner. In an environment where those different from us are treated as enemies, we recognize them as fellow human beings, treat them with dignity and care, and embrace them as friends.

Jesus himself was a displaced person, fleeing as a child with his family to Egypt to escape a ruler's violence. He told parables that cast despised foreigners as heroes and taught that welcoming the stranger is the same as welcoming him.

Hospitality isn't a soft virtue; it's a prophetic act.[118]

Welcoming people into our lives, homes, families, churches, cities, towns, and nations isn't easy, and it isn't the way human beings are naturally wired. We tend to exclude, demonize, and scapegoat those who are different from us. Yet, Christian hospitality declares that our identity isn't in our passport but in our baptism, not in our blood but in our shared humanity. Hospitality subverts the fear-driven narratives of nationalism by embodying the kingdom's expansive inclusion, welcome, and love.

---

[118] Claiborne and Haw, *Jesus for President.*

Worship Without Idols

Nationalism demands liturgies: pledges, anthems, symbols, and rituals that form the heart's loyalties. Christian nationalism co-opts the church's worship, blending patriotic ceremony with praise until the distinction between God and country blurs. Such nationalism is an idol demanding blood, allegiance, and worship, and to give it these things is to commit idolatry (to worship a false god).

True worship resists this fusion. It gathers believers around bread and wine, not banners and slogans. It centers on the story of a crucified and risen Lord, not the myths of national greatness.

When we worship the Lamb, we're reminded that every tribe, tongue, and nation will stand together before the throne. No single nation will dominate that gathering. The vision is polyvocal, multicultural, and united not by language or law but by the love of Christ.

Nonviolence and the Way of the Cross

Christian nationalism often justifies violence, whether in foreign wars, domestic policing, control of institutions, or suppression of dissent, as necessary for preserving the nation's way of life. But the gospel calls us to a different logic.

The cross is the ultimate act of nonviolence: absorbing violence without returning it, overcoming evil with good. To follow Jesus is to reject the myth that peace can be secured through the sword. Where Christian nationalism justifies violence, control, and homogenization as a means to peace and order, Jesus calls us to honor and celebrate peacemaking, compassion, diversity, and human freedom and dignity.

Peacemaking doesn't mean passivity. Active peacemaking involves speaking up courageously, stepping out into risky situations, confronting injustice without dehumanizing the oppressor, and resisting evil without mirroring it. Peacemaking means seeing the image of God in those nationalism calls "enemy" and seeking their good.

The Church as an Alternative Polis

The church isn't the chaplain of the state. It's an alternative community, a polis shaped by the beatitudes, nourished by the sacraments, and ordered by the law of love.[119]

When the church aligns itself with nationalist politics, it loses its prophetic voice. It becomes an echo of the state rather than a sign of the kingdom. However, when it exists as a distinct community, characterized by generosity, reconciliation, and justice, it offers the world a glimpse of a better way.

Christian spirituality invites us to see the church not as a voting bloc but as a pilgrim people. We're strangers and exiles on the earth, seeking a city whose architect and builder is God. Our task is to live now as if that city were already here.

Cruciform Allegiance

The crucifixion is the ultimate test of allegiance. Will we follow the one who is lifted up in glory or the one lifted up on a cross? Will we serve the power that kills in order to win, or the power that dies in order to love?

Christian nationalism can't make sense of a Messiah who refuses to conquer Rome, who rides into Jerusalem on a donkey, who washes feet, who spends time with the broken and lowly, who pours out his blood for the sake of strangers and enemies, and who tells his followers to put away their swords. But this is the scandal and the wisdom of the cross: the belief that love is stronger than death, that vulnerability is greater than control, that embrace triumphs over exclusion, and that humility is more powerful than empire.

"The kingdom of God doesn't come wrapped in a flag. It comes wrapped in a towel, washing the feet of the world."

---

[119] Hauerwas, *Resident Aliens.*

The Mystical Vision Beyond Borders

Christian mystics have always known that our true homeland is God. They speak of union with the Divine as the ultimate belonging, a reality that makes every earthly identity secondary.

In this vision, borders become temporary lines in the sand, and national distinctions fade in the light of eternal love. The soul learns to see the other not as foreign but as kin, not as a threat but as a gift. Christian creeds, prayers, contemplation, worship, liturgies, and Scripture lift our eyes above borders, flags, walls, politics, partisanship, and nations.

Christian nationalism thrives on fear of the other. Christian spirituality thrives on communion with the other, and on the union of hearts made possible by the astonishing sacrifice and love of God, revealed in Jesus Christ. Christian discipleship invites us to step into the vast, borderless expanse of God's kingdom, where the only passport is faith, hope, and love.

A Call to Repentance

The way of Jesus always begins with repentance. For those entangled in Christian nationalism, this means confessing the ways we've confused God with country, faith with ideology, discipleship with flag, and mission with political conquest.

It means turning from fear to trust, from control to surrender, and from exclusion to embrace. It means laying down the sword, the banner, and the myth of exceptionalism to take up the cross.

Repentance isn't shame. It's liberation. It frees us to live as citizens of the kingdom, no longer bound by the demands of nationalism but empowered by the Spirit to love without limits.

Living the Kingdom Now

The alternative to Christian nationalism isn't political withdrawal but kingdom engagement. It's living here and now as ambassadors of a realm that has no borders and knows no end.

This means advocating for policies that reflect kingdom values: justice for people experiencing poverty, protection for the vulnerable, welcome for the stranger, care for creation, and peacemaking in a violent world. It means resisting any ideology, left or right, that compromises the gospel for the sake of power.

Above all, it means living in such a way that people see in us the character of Christ: humility, compassion, courage, and truth.

Christ Above All

Christian nationalism fails because it asks too little of us and calls us to a wrong set of priorities and allegiances. It trades the expansive vision of God's kingdom for the narrow confines of national interest.

Christian nationalism invites us to love our own but not our enemies, to seek security but not the cross, to pursue greatness but not goodness. It teaches us to bless those who look like us while ignoring the stranger at the gate, to protect our comforts while neglecting the vulnerable, to raise flags higher than we bend knees, to confuse political triumph with spiritual faithfulness, and to value the preservation of power over the practice of mercy. It tempts us to trade the upside-down kingdom for a kingdom of our own making, one where battle cries replace the Beatitudes, and the way of Jesus is overshadowed by the will to dominate. It calls us to win at any cost but not to lose our lives for Christ's sake, to conquer through might but not to overcome through love, to proclaim our nation's glory but not the glory of the cross, and to draw boundaries where Jesus tore down dividing walls.

Discipleship and allegiance to Jesus Christ call us to a higher and deeper level than Christian nationalism.

Christian nationalism clings to borders; Christ's kingdom breaks them down.

Christian nationalism guards its own; Christ's kingdom welcomes the stranger.

Christian nationalism seeks power; Christ's kingdom pours it out.

Christian nationalism rallies under a flag; Christ's kingdom gathers at a table.

Christian nationalism promises safety; Christ's kingdom calls us into sacrifice.

Christian nationalism builds walls; Christ's kingdom washes feet.

Christian nationalism prizes dominance; Christ's kingdom delights in mercy.

Christian nationalism exalts a nation; Christ's kingdom exalts the cross.

The One we follow was crucified outside the city gates, rejected by the powers of both state and temple, yet risen to break the grip of death. This King reigns over every nation yet calls us friends, summoning us to a loyalty that transcends all earthly allegiances and a love that encompasses the whole world. Our task is clear: to live as citizens of heaven, ambassadors of reconciliation, bearers of a kingdom that can't be shaken. And when the flags are folded and the nations pass away, God's glory, Christ's love, the Spirit's presence, and the kingdom of heaven will remain.

"Only one kingdom lasts forever, and it's not built by human hands."

Epilogue: The Kingdom Without Banners

The flags still wave. The news still scrolls. The noise of allegiance still fills the air. Nations rise and fall; the powerful still speak in thunder. Yet for those who've glimpsed the crucified Christ, everything has changed. The symbols that once dazzled now fade beside a greater light. The idols of tribe and pride, of race and border, stand exposed before a kingdom that can't be mapped or militarized. The One who died outside the city walls still reigns: supremely, eternally, mercifully, and from a throne and the margins.

God's grace moves through the wreckage of empire. It shows up not in parades but in bread shared across divides, in forgiveness that refuses to bow to fear, in the slow courage of those who choose peace when vengeance would be easier. The reign of Christ doesn't arrive through conquest; it breaks in like dawn: mercifully, insistent, unstoppable. Every act of compassion becomes its herald. Every table opened to the stranger becomes its altar. Every refusal to worship power becomes a protest against it.

This is the beginning of holy sight. To live as disciples without flags is to walk through the world awake: to see divine light shimmering on faces the world has taught us to despise, to carry the scent of heaven into the dust of politics and pain, to speak mercy in the language of justice and justice in the language of love. It's to believe that even in the ruins, resurrection is already at work.

The call is the same as it has always been: to follow the One who emptied glory to dwell among the broken, who exchanged titles for towels, and whose throne is shaped like a cross. The kingdom that outlasts every nation isn't built by might or decree but by those who dare to love in a loveless time.

So as these pages close, lift your eyes. The world still longs and groans, but Christ still walks among us: unarmed, unflagged, unmatched, undefeated. The Spirit still broods over chaos, still speaks creation into being, still calls us to join the revolution of faith, hope, and love.

The kingdom isn't coming someday.

It's already here:

in the wound that forgives,

in the stranger who's welcomed,

in the courage to bless those who curse,

in the cross that still outshines every flag.

Bibliography

Akaeze, Anthony. "Fire from Africa: The Influence of 'Reverse Missions' Today." *Baptist News Global.* March 23, 2021. https://baptistnews.com/article/fire-from-africa-the-influence-of-reverse-missions-today/

Anyabwile, Thabiti. "Doug Wilson's Views on Race, Racism, Slavery and the Bible." *The Gospel Coalition*, March 13, 2013. https://www.thegospelcoalition.org/blogs/thabiti-anyabwile/doug-wilsons-views-on-race-racism-slavery-and-the-bible/

Athanasius. *On the Incarnation.* Translated by John Behr. Yonkers: St. Vladimir's Seminary, 2011.

Barrett, Frank J. "Organizational Dynamics: Creating Appreciative Learning Cultures." *American Management Association* (1995).

Bookless, Dave, et al. "Creation Care." *Lausanne Movement.* Accessed September 1, 2025. https://lausanne.org/report/sustainable/creation-care

Bosch, David J. *A Spirituality of the Road.* Scottdale: Herald, 1979.

Branson, Mark Lau. *Memories, Hopes, and Conversations: Appreciative Inquiry and Congregational Change.* Herndon: Alban, 2004.

Brown, Juanita, and David Isaacs. *The World Café: Shaping Our Futures through Conversations That Matter.* 1st Ed. San Francisco: Berrett-Koehler, 2005.

Brueggemann, Walter. *The Message of the Psalms: A Theological Commentary.* Minneapolis: Augsburg Fortress, 1984.

Carter, Warren. *Matthew and the Margins: A Sociopolitical and Religious Reading.* Maryknoll: Orbis, 2000.

Cavanaugh, William T., *Migrations of the Holy: God, State, and the Political Meaning of the Church*. Grand Rapids: Eerdmans, 2011.

Cheng-Tozun, Dorcas. "What Majority-World Missions Really Looks Like." *Christianity Today*. August 26, 2019. https://www.christianitytoday.com/2019/08/what-majority-world-missions-really-looks-like/

Christian, Jayakumar. "Rise of the Urban Poor," in Graham Joseph Hill (ed.) *Signs of Hope in the City: Renewing Urban Mission, Embracing Radical Hope*. Melbourne: ISUM, 2015.

Claiborne, Shane and Chris Haw, *Jesus for President: Politics for Ordinary Radicals*. Grand Rapids: Zondervan, 2008.

Costas, Orlando E. *Christ Outside the Gate: Mission beyond Christendom*. Maryknoll: Orbis, 1982.

Equal Justice Initiative. "Racial Justice." Accessed August 25, 2025. https://eji.org/racial-justice/

Garrison, David. *Church Planting Movements*. Richmond: International Missions Board, 1999. Accessed September 1, 2025. https://moredisciples.com/wp-content/uploads/2016/01/cpm_booklet_standard_english.pdf

Gorski, Philip and Samuel L. Perry, *The Flag and the Cross: White Christian Nationalism and the Threat to American Democracy*. New York: Oxford University Press, 2022.

Grace Communion International. "A Slave as a Brother (Philemon 1–21)." Accessed August 25, 2025. https://www.gci.org/articles/philemon-a-slave-as-a-brother/

Gutiérrez, Gustavo. *A Theology of Liberation: History, Politics, and Salvation*. Maryknoll: Orbis, 1988.

Hauerwas, Stanley, *Resident Aliens: Life in the Christian Colony*. Nashville: Abingdon, 1989.

Hearth, Katey. "Christian Population Rises Nearly 40 Percent in Nepal." July 4, 2023. *Mission Network News*. https://www.mnnonline.org/news/christian-population-rises-nearly-40-percent-in-nepal/

Hill, Graham Joseph. *World Christianity: An Introduction*. Eugene: Cascade, 2024.

Hoppe, Reed. "6 Stories of God's Holy Spirit, Fresh from the Mission Field." November 11, 2016. *TMS Global*. https://www.tms-global.org/story-details/6-stories-of-gods-holy-spirit-fresh-from-the-mission-field

International Labor Organization. "50 Million People in Modern Slavery." September 12, 2022. https://www.ilo.org/resource/news/50-million-people-worldwide-modern-slavery-0

Jenkins, Philip. *The Next Christendom: The Coming of Global Christianity*. 3rd Ed. Oxford: Oxford University Press, 2011.

Johnson, Kevin Rashid. "Prison Labor Is Modern Slavery. I've Been Sent to Solitary for Speaking Out." *The Guardian*, August 23, 2018. https://www.theguardian.com/commentisfree/2018/aug/23/pris oner-speak-out-american-slave-labor-strike

Kim, Justin. "Embracing Digital Evangelism." *Digital Missionary*. January 30, 2024. https://www.dmissionary.com/post/chapter-1-embracing-digital-evangelism

King, Martin Luther, Jr. *"Remaining Awake Through a Great Revolution."* Sermon delivered at the National Cathedral, Washington, March 31, 1968. (Printed in *A Testament of Hope: The Essential Writings and Speeches of Martin Luther King, Jr.*, edited by James M. Washington, 1986). https://kinginstitute.stanford.edu/king-papers/documents/remaining-awake-through-great-revolution-address-morehouse-college

Kiser, Charles. "David Watson and Church Planting Movements." May 18, 2009. *In The Storyline*. https://inthestoryline.com/2009/05/18/david-watson-and-church-planting-movements/

Kuo, Lily. "Africa's 'Reverse Missionaries' are Bringing Christianity Back to the United Kingdom." *Quartz*. July 21, 2017.

https://qz.com/africa/1088489/africas-reverse-missionaries-are-trying-to-bring-christianity-back-to-the-united-kingdom

Levendusky, Matthew. *How Partisan Media Polarize America.* Chicago: University of Chicago Press, 2013.

Levitsky, Steven, and Daniel Ziblatt, *How Democracies Die.* Danvers: Crown, 2018.

Lewis, John. Interview by Kim Lawton. *"John Lewis Extended Interview." Religion & Ethics NewsWeekly.* PBS, January 16, 2004. https://www.pbs.org/wnet/religionandethics/2004/01/16/january-16-2004-john-lewis-extended-interview/2897/

McCracken, Brett. "21 Challenges Facing the 21st Century Church." *BrettMcCracken.com* (blog), October 27, 2016. https://www.brettmccracken.com/blog/blog/2016/10/27/21-challenges-facing-the-21st-century-church

McKnight, Scot, *Kingdom Conspiracy: Returning to the Radical Mission of the Local Church.* Grand Rapids: Brazos, 2014.

Merton, Thomas. *New Seeds of Contemplation.* New York: New Directions, 1961.

Miller, Paul D., *The Religion of American Greatness: What's Wrong with Christian Nationalism.* Downers Grove: IVP Academic, 2022.

Moltmann, Jürgen. *The Crucified God: The Cross of Christ as the Foundation and Criticism of Christian Theology.* Minneapolis: Fortress, 1993.

Nouwen, Henri J.M. *Life of the Beloved: Spiritual Living in a Secular World.* New York: Crossroad, 1992.

Ott, Craig, and Harold A. Netland. *Globalizing Theology: Belief and Practice in an Era of World Christianity.* Grand Rapids: Baker Academic, 2006.

Padilla, C. René. "The Contextualization of the Gospel." *Journal of Theology for Southern Africa,* no. 24 (1978).

Pearse, Roger. "A Fuller Extract from Gregory of Nyssa on the Evils of Slavery." January 24, 2019. https://www.roger-pearse.com/weblog/2019/01/24/a-fuller-extract-from-gregory-of-nyssa-on-the-evils-of-slavery/

Pohl, Christine D. *Making Room: Recovering Hospitality as a Christian Tradition.* Grand Rapids: Eerdmans, 1999.

Randall, Rebecca. "Preaching That Connects Creation Care to Climate Change." March 5, 2024. *Science for the Church.* https://scienceforthechurch.org/2024/03/05/preaching-that-connects-creation-care-to-climate-change/

Robert's Blog. "Two Frederick Douglass Quotes." February 6, 2017. https://www.raterrell.com/2017/02/06/two-frederick-douglass-quotes/

Sanchez, Michelle T. "What We Can Learn from the Contemplative Heart of the Civil Rights Movement." *Faith & Leadership* (Duke Divinity School), March 19, 2024. https://faithandleadership.com/what-we-can-learn-the-contemplative-heart-the-civil-rights-movement

Tearfund USA. "How Integral Mission Creates Lasting Change." *Tearfund USA.* August 25, 2023. https://www.tearfundusa.org/integral_mission_blog

Teresa of Ávila. *The Interior Castle.* Translated by Mirabai Starr. New York: Riverhead, 2003.

The New Oxford Annotated Bible: New Revised Standard Version with the Apocrypha. Edited by Michael D. Coogan. 5th ed. New York: Oxford University Press, 2018.

The UNESCO Courier. "The Deep Legacy of Slavery." March 28, 2025. https://courier.unesco.org/en/articles/deep-legacy-slavery

Thurman, Howard. *Jesus and the Disinherited.* New York: Abingdon-Cokesbury, 1949.

Thurman, Howard. *Meditations of the Heart.* New York: Harper & Brothers, 1953.

Tizon, Al. *Transformation after Lausanne: Radical Evangelical Mission in Global-Local Perspective.* Eugene: Wipf and Stock, 2008.

Tornkvist, Karen J. *Sanctuary: The Traditions and Possibilities.* Philadelphia: Fortress, 1992.

Vicari, Chelsen. "7 Sojourner Truth Quotes on Equality Grounded in Faith." *Juicy Ecumenism*, February 13, 2017. https://juicyecumenism.com/2017/02/13/7-sojourner-truth-quotes-equality-grounded-faith/

Watkins, Jane Magruder, and Bernard J. Mohr. *Appreciative Inquiry: Change at the Speed of Imagination.* Practicing Organization Development Series. 2nd Ed. San Francisco: Pfeiffer, 2011.

Werntz, Myles. "Howard Thurman's Contemplative Nonviolence." *The Christian Century*, August 28, 2019. https://www.christiancentury.org/critical-essay/howard-thurman-s-contemplative-nonviolence

Whitehead, Andrew L. and Samuel L. Perry, *Taking America Back for God: Christian Nationalism in the United States.* New York: Oxford University Press, 2020.

Whitney, Diana Kaplin, and Amanda Trosten-Bloom. *The Power of Appreciative Inquiry: A Practical Guide to Positive Change.* 1st Ed. San Francisco: Berrett-Koehler, 2003.

Wikipedia, "Indigenous Church Mission Theory." Accessed September 1, 2025. https://en.wikipedia.org/wiki/Indigenous_church_mission_theory

Willesden, Savannah. "A Fresh Expression of Church: Something New that Reminds Us of Old." Accessed September 1, 2025. *Faithward.* https://www.faithward.org/a-fresh-expression-of-church-something-new-that-reminds-us-of-old/

Wolterstorff, Nicholas. *Justice in Love.* Grand Rapids: Eerdmans, 2011.

Wright, N. T. *Jesus and the Victory of God.* Minneapolis: Fortress, 1996.

Wright, N. T., *How God Became King: The Forgotten Story of the Gospels.* New York: HarperOne, 2012.

YWAM Salem. "How Refugees Transform Christianity: Biblical & Ministry Stories." *YWAM Salem.* November 4, 2024. https://www.ywamsalem.org/blog/gods-purpose-in-the-movement-of-people-how-refugees-shape-the-gospel-story

Appendix 1: Discussion Guide

The Israel–Gaza War

1. Where do you see Christ's presence in the midst of violence, suffering, and geopolitical conflict?
2. How can lament become an act of faith rather than despair when confronting war and injustice?
3. In what ways might Christians hold together solidarity with the oppressed and compassion for all sides in a conflict?
4. What does it mean for the church to be a peacemaking body in a world addicted to retaliation and fear?
5. How can we embody hope in situations that seem beyond redemption?

Undocumented Immigrants

1. How does the story of Jesus's own displacement and refugee status shape our view of migrants and asylum seekers today?
2. What fears or assumptions about immigration might God be inviting you (or your community) to surrender?
3. How can local churches become places of sanctuary, hospitality, and advocacy for the undocumented?
4. What practices help you recognize the image of God in those who live on society's margins?
5. In what ways might the movement of peoples across borders be a sign of God's mission in the world?

The Wounds That See

1. Why do some Christians view empathy with suspicion, and how might the cross challenge those fears?
2. What does "cruciform empathy" look like in your daily life, especially when someone's pain or viewpoint unsettles you?
3. How can empathy be both compassionate and discerning, tender without losing truth?
4. When have you experienced another's empathy as a healing presence?
5. How might the church become a school of empathy in a world numbed by outrage and indifference?

Slavery, Freedom, and the Crucified Christ

1. How does the cross speak to histories of oppression, slavery, and systemic injustice?
2. What can contemporary believers learn from the faith and resilience of enslaved Christians who found liberation in the crucified Christ?
3. In what ways does remembering the cross through the lens of the oppressed purify and expand our theology?
4. How might we confront modern forms of slavery (economic, racial, or spiritual) in our own contexts?
5. What does true freedom look like when measured by the life and love of Jesus rather than by cultural definitions?

What is Christian Mission?

1. If the church "exists by mission as fire exists by burning," what might it mean for your local church to recover this sense of identity and purpose?
2. Why do you think the word mission has become so vague in modern Christianity, and what dangers arise when mission is shaped more by culture or ideology than by Scripture?

3. How does the idea of joining God's redemptive work shift our understanding of mission from something we do for God to something we do with God?

4. The definition you offer describes mission as "integral," combining word, sign, and deed. Where do you see imbalances in today's church, where one of these dimensions dominates or is neglected?

5. What excites or challenges you about the idea that mission is now "from everywhere to everywhere"? How does this reframe traditional ideas of sending, leadership, and partnership across cultures?

Christian Spirituality and Theology in a New Urban World

1. Where do you see local stories in your city needing to meet global voices (and vice versa) to form a truly "glocal" theology and spirituality? What concrete table could you set this month to make that exchange real?

2. In your context, what would it look like to practice prayer, Scripture, worship, and ethics that immerse you in the city's wounds (poverty, racism, exploitation) rather than retreat from them?

3. Which Majority World, Indigenous, or First Nations voices do you need to learn from right now? How will you reorder time, budget, and platforms so those voices don't just inform but shape your church's urban discipleship?

4. Name two "appreciative" practices (e.g., Appreciative Inquiry/World Café) your community could adopt to notice grace, harvest collective wisdom, and keep hope alive in dense, exhausting urban realities.

5. Where is your church currently on this journey in your neighborhood? What specific next step would move you toward a reconciled community (e.g., shared meals, legal aid, language

classes, trauma-aware pastoral care, youth apprenticeships), and who will lead it?

Missions on the Move

1. Which of the ten global shifts in mission most inspires or challenges your understanding of the church's future?
2. How does recognizing Christianity as a worldwide, polycentric movement reshape Western ideas of "sending" and "receiving"?
3. Where do you see God at work in digital spaces, migration flows, or environmental movements today?
4. What does it mean to practice "mission beyond empire": collaborative, humble, and locally led?
5. How might your own community participate more faithfully in God's global mission of justice, reconciliation, and creation care?

Activism with a Monk's Heart

1. Why do prayer and protest need each other, and what happens when they're separated?
2. How does the example of Howard Thurman (and those he influenced) reframe what it means to pursue justice from a place of peace?
3. What personal practices help you "center down" amid exhaustion, anger, or despair in your own activism or ministry?
4. How can communities of faith cultivate rhythms that sustain justice work for the long haul?
5. What would it look like to love your adversaries without excusing their injustice?

A Spiritual Path Beyond Toxic Politics

1. In what ways has political polarization shaped your own heart or relationships?
2. What does it mean to treat democracy as a spiritual practice rather than merely a political system?

3. How can curiosity, confession, and silence become antidotes to outrage?
4. What small actions could you take to restore trust, humility, and empathy in your civic life or community?
5. How does the gospel call us to love across ideological divides without surrendering conviction?

Christ Without a Flag: The Kingdom Beyond Nationalism

1. How has nationalism or cultural identity influenced your understanding of faith and discipleship?
2. What does it mean to follow a Savior who belongs to no nation yet loves every nation?
3. Where do you see the church confusing allegiance to Christ with allegiance to power or nation?
4. How might Christians witness to a kingdom that transcends all borders, parties, and flags?
5. What practical commitments can help us live as citizens of God's borderless reign here and now?

Appendix 2: Would You Help?

Writing a book takes immense effort. It's a sustained labor of love over months, even years. Every page carries hours of thought, prayer, revision, and hope. And while the writing may be solitary, the life of a book is communal. That's where you come in. If this book has meant something to you, I'd be deeply grateful if you could help it find its way into more hands and hearts.

There are two simple but powerful ways you can do that.

First, consider leaving a short review on Amazon (and Goodreads would be wonderful too). Even just a few sentences can help others discover the book, as reviews significantly influence how books are recommended and shared online. You can do that by visiting Amazon or searching for this book and writing a review. Even a short note helps people find the book.

Second, if the book has stirred something in you, would you share it with others: friends, groups, churches, or anyone who might benefit from its message?

Your support helps keep this work going, and it means more than I can say. Thank you for being part of this journey.

Find this book on these pages:
1. Amazon:
https://www.amazon.com.au/stores/author/B008NI4ORQ
2. Goodreads:
https://www.goodreads.com/author/show/20347171.Graham_Joseph_Hill

3. Author Website:
https://grahamjosephhill.com/books/

Appendix 3: About Me

Graham Joseph Hill (OAM, PhD) is an Adjunct Research Fellow and Associate Professor at Charles Sturt University, and one of Australia's most prolific and awarded Christian authors. He's written more than twenty books, including *Salt, Light, and a City*, which was named Jesus Creed's 2012 Book of the Year (church category); *Healing Our Broken Humanity* (with Grace Ji-Sun Kim), named Outreach Magazine's 2019 Resource of the Year (culture category); and *World Christianity*, shortlisted for the 2025 Australian Christian Book of the Year. In 2024, Graham was awarded the Medal of the Order of Australia (OAM) for his service to theological education. He lives in Sydney with his wife, Shyn.

Author and Ministry Websites

GrahamJosephHill.com
GrahamJosephHill.Substack.com
youtube.com/@GrahamJosephHill_Author
Linktr.ee/dailydevotions
facebook.com/grahamjosephhill/
instagram.com/grahamjosephhill/
amazon.com.au/stores/author/B008NI4ORQ
goodreads.com/author/show/20347171.Graham_Joseph_Hill

Books

See all my books at GrahamJosephHill.com/books

Appendix 4: Connect With Me

I'd love to stay connected with you. You can sign up to my Substack, Spirituality and Society with Hilly, where I share new writing, spiritual reflections, and updates on future books. Please find me on Substack: https://grahamjosephhill.substack.com

You can also find my books on my website: https://grahamjosephhill.com/books

You can also connect with me through my Facebook author page: https://www.facebook.com/GrahamJosephHill/